CHINA WATCHER

THE KOREA TIMES

By Jaeho Hwang

CHINA WATCHER

By Jaeho Hwang

Cover design by HyeJin Cho
Design edited by People Communication (+82-2-6713-8790)
Edited by Sunho Shin, ByeongCheol Lee
Printed by Twinbell (+82-2-2088-1810)

Published in Republic of Korea by Huine, an imprint of Hankuk University of Foreign Studies University Knowledge Contents and Press, Seoul.

http://press.hufs.ac.kr

First printing, January 17th, 2020

ISBN 979-11-5901-665-3 03340
Price 20,000 Won

CHINA WATCHER

Seeking Common Grounds while Narrowing Differences

In collaboration with THE KOREA TIMES

By Jaeho Hwang

CHINESE DIPLOMACY

—

KOREAN DIPLOMACY

—

PUBLIC DIPLOMACY

HU:iNE

Contents

Introduction

I have been personally contributing to The Korea Times for a while. Later I and Publisher Oh Young-jin from the Korea Times had a few serious talks regarding Korea's foreign policy and Korea-China relations. While Korea-China relations were facing a hard time, we thought of making efforts to improve the relationship as in the news media level. That was the summer of 2017, when Terminal High Altitude Area Defense (THAAD) was coming as a major challenge to bilateral relations.

When our minds were set, the next steps flowed rapid from then on. We first started with opening a section titled "China Watcher" in the Korea Times website. It covers all the issues that are directly or indirectly related to China, from the perspectives and voices of Koreans, Chinese, and other foreigners. The corner is largely divided into views, reviews and interviews. China Watcher's banner shows Dragon and Tiananmen Square, which symbolizes China. The dragon represents the holy spirit in Chinese mythology and Tiananmen Square shows the modern New China.

More than 70 articles have been contributed in the past two years, since the first one on November 14, 2017. It was published every week except for some time during the summer and winter breaks. The authors are from all around the world, mostly from Korea, China, and Japan. Total

34 views, 10 reviews, and 28 interviews were written. The topics also varied, but can be largely distinguished into three parts: Chinese Diplomacy, Korean Diplomacy, and Public Diplomacy.

This book introduces 46 articles. Part Ⅰ 'China's Foreign Relations' covers China's Foreign Policy and the relations between China and the United States, China and the Korean Peninsula, China and its other neighbors with 13 articles. Part Ⅱ 'Korea's Foreign Relations' is consisted of 18 articles of Korea's diplomatic relations with China, the United States, Japan and other neighboring countries. Part Ⅲ 'The Public Diplomacy' deals with issues such as universities, locals and enterprises, language and communication, and multicultural society with total 15 articles. The contributors and interviewees have wide spectrum from senior government officials, professors, think-tanks, to ordinary people and students.

The book will be a supportive reference for the students, people, and foreigners who are interested in Korea-China relations. Especially, interviews with China's a vice chairperson of the National People's Congress Foreign Affairs Committee Fu Ying, Chinese Ambassador to Korea Qiu Guohong, Party Secretary of the Shanghai International Studies University Jiang Feng, South Korea's Deputy Foreign Minister Yoon Soon-gu, and

Japanese Ambassador to Seoul Yasumasa Nagamine will be greatly helpful in understanding the foreign policies of the Korea, China, and Japan.

While working on this book, I thank Director Oh Young-jin, who not only recognized the value of China Watcher and fully supported without any hesitation, but also suggested to publish the articles into a book. Also, I appreciate web designer Lee Jong-eun and reporter Dong Sun-hwa at The Korea Times for designing wonderful banner and managing China Watcher section every week. I also deliver my gratitude to my students as well as the researchers of Global Security Cooperation Center in Hankuk University of Foreign Studies, Ko Sung-hwah and Song Min-joo, who assisted with translation. In particular, thanks to Sung-hwah for being along from the beginning to the very end in publishing this book.

If you take a closer look at the China Watcher banner, it says "Seeking Common Ground while Narrowing Differences". Many Korea-China conversations between the governments, think tanks, and in private level conclude by saying Qiú tónghuà yì (to find common ground, leaving behind the differences). It is correct, but it sometimes gives a passive impression. The higher Korea-China relations develop, the more active attitude is required. Only when the differences are narrowed down, Korea-China relations can truly take a leap forward.

This year marked the 70th anniversary of China's founding. In the meantime, China has evolved from an Asian patient to the strong man. During the period, Korea has become a middle power in Asia. Since the establishment of diplomatic relations in 1992, Korea and China together have been improved for last 27 years. This little book might cannot talk a lot or explain many things about Korea-China relations, but if someone newly find perspectives and understandings on Korea-China relations and get interested in its future, publishing this book will be meaningful already. That will be my personal best, along with the appreciation of those who have contributed to this book.

January, 2020

Professor Jaeho Hwang, PhD

Director, Global Security Cooperation Center

Hankuk University of Foreign Studies Seoul Campus

Congratulatory message

China is a strong neighbor to Korea. Before the Cold War, China could not have an influence on Korea's foreign affairs and security environment. Since the establishment of diplomatic relations in August 1992, however, China has become an inseparable relationship in Korea's security and economy. The United States, on the other hand, as the existing ally, is in an absolute relationship to Korea. This is the fact in East Asia, or at least on the Korean Peninsula, as the term G2 stands for the two powers, the United State and China.

Two years ago, The Korea Times was the media outlet that desired to observe China. The media is an appropriate way to follow up on every move of China. However, there is a limit in observing China in a long perspective, analyze on certain issues, and to interesting views from various perspectives.

In this time, by chance, I met professor Jaeho Hwang from Division of International Studies at Hankuk University of Foreign Studies. As we shared thoughts, we could reach a point to create the 'China Watcher' column on the website of The Korea Times. The plan was to open a space where people from various fields, including government officials, diplomats, businessmen, and even ordinary people and students, can contribute.

In the beginning, professor Hwang mentioned the goal to contribute one article every week, however, I personally concerned if it would be possible. This is because once a week is never easy. It requires finding the contributors, interviewees, and work in English. Now I can tell this was an unnecessary concern. Over the past two years, more than 70 articles have been well published.

I suggested professor Hwang that it is important to share these meaningful works online, but what if we could publish it offline. It would be very significant to make a physical book in offline space, since it will be realizing the memories into a vivid reality. I have no doubt that this book will be a great opportunity for foreigners, students, and English speaking citizens to understand Korea's perspective on China. We look forward to meeting China Watcher, the second volume.

Oh Young-jin
The Korea Times Publisher
2019. 12. 6

Baotou
Beijing
(Peking)
Tianjin
Taiyuan
Jinan
Fenyang
Huang He
(Yellow)
Zhengzhou
Xi'an
N
A
Han
Wuhan
Yichang
Chongqing

I

China's Foreign Relations

China Watcher

1. 1. China's Foreign Policy

[INTERVIEW]

Desire to share China's experience with the International Community

With Fu Ying, Vice chairperson, Foreign Affairs Committee in National People's Congress, China.

By Jaeho Hwang

In the early October, I met with Fu Ying, the current Vice chairperson (Vice Minister in terms of Korea) of the Foreign Affairs Committee in National People's Congress. Fu Ying is one of the most famous Chinese in the world. Her name often comes with the word "First in China". She was the first female vice foreign minister since the reform and opening in 1978, the first Chinese female Ambassador to Australia and the UK, and the first female spokesman of National People's Congress, which is the same concept as the National Assembly of Korea.

Currently, she is the Honorary Dean of the Institute of International Relations of Tsinghua University and Chairperson of the Center for International Strategy and Security (CISS). In addition, according to a 2019 Report by the Hoover Institution of Stanford University, Fu Ying is highly evaluated as the "Senior figure in a growing number of US-China interactions". Recently, she also published an English book "Seeing the World". She is closely related to Korea, therefore, participated in the six-party talks as the director of the Foreign Ministry, and enjoys Korean dramas such as Daejanggeum. Personally, she drinks suutei tsai (Hohhot-style milk tea) on the weekends, listens to the traditional Mongol long song.

Q. First, would you explain the meaning of the 70th anniversary China's National Foundation Day?

A. Under the leadership of the Communist Party of China, with the efforts of the Chinese people, China has escaped the poverty is now the second largest economy in the world. China's global influence has grown and is increasingly playing a role in international affairs. What the international community cannot but acknowledge, whether it is for or against China's achievements, is that China's system and governance eventually is successful. China's success, in other words, means to rewrite the Western-led international political and economic textbooks, and it is worth to be referred as a model for the realization of civilization pursued by mankind.

Q. How are you observing the rise of China?

A. China that is on the rise while US in retreat constitute a major driving force behind a new round of adjustment in the world power structure. China's economic success has captured the imagination of the world. Thanks to sustained and rapid economic growth, Chinese living standards have been materially improved, and China now boasts full-fledged infrastructure and a manufacturing sector of depth and width. China's influence is also on the rise in terms of its system, culture, military and in other domains, thus giving China more voice and weight in international affairs.

Q. How will China's rise affect the international community?

A. China pursues peaceful rise within the existing world order and global system, and it has a lot of stake in upholding it. But it also needs to tackle squarely the unjust, irrational and anachronistic aspects of the system, and take vigorous actions to reform and improve global governance. By virtue of natural endowment and late-comer advantage, China is well placed to play a more important role, and empowers world economic growth with the Belt and Road initiative, and ultimately grow out of the old world system and embrace a new one that encourages peaceful co-existence, common prosperity and the building of a community with a shared future for humanity. Only by making more tangible contributions to improving global governance can China lend credence to the logic that when China gets stronger, the peace, development and prosperity of the world are better safeguarded.

Q. What kind of policies and efforts should China have to achieve this?

A. China still is a developing country and the road to building a comprehensive national power is yet a long way off. China, however, is achieving a world-recognizable modernization outcome and wants to share Chinese style of development methods and experiences with the international community,

instead of ending up as just China's own. We are willing to introduce China's development and achievements to the international community through the voice of the Chinese, the writings, and books of the Chinese people. Therefore, we should strengthen the international news media industry, which can deliver it as well as the Western has gone through. China can also take the lead in international opinion by strengthening its Agenda setting ability and the ability to lead the discourse of international voices. Eventually, creating a discourse in the international community will assist China to enhance China's positive international status and shape.

Q. Would you share your perspective on the US leadership?

A. Though the US is a dominant power in the world, its strategic miscalculation and misguided policies have eroded its global clout and standing, overstretched its financial means, hence weakening its willingness to stay at the helm of world affairs. Under the Trump presidency, the US has been cutting back commitment to external affairs, jumping at every opportunity to unload nonessential obligations in order to avoid getting mired in any regional conflicts. As such, even though the US still manages to preserve its supremacy, probably its hegemony has passed its heyday.

Q. Will how China-US relations evolve shape global political architecture in the years ahead?

A. The "Power transition" theory envisions that the established power would not readily relinquish power to the rising power, while the rising power will use its rapidly accrued strength to explore overseas markets, build up military power, monopolize cutting-edge technologies, and purge the established power, all aiming to change the existing order and norms and attain global privilege that is on par with its new found power, which means upending the old order. When the rising power unseats the established power and thus completes the transition, it marks the onset of a new world order. History suggests that "Power transition" in modern times took place invariably between western powers and fierce competition was a hallmark, though they hailed from more or less the same history, culture and system. So here the "Power transition" in its essence is leadership transition within one and the same political and civilization ecosystem.

Q. Artificial Intelligence (AI) is a global topic these days. How will AI impact the international order?

A. In terms of the international configuration, AI may shift the balance of economic and military power among countries, empower the non-state actors in an unprecedented way and intensify international technological competition. With regard to international norms, AI is likely to change the forms and principles of war, thus exerting an impact on the existing international laws and ethics. The security and governance challenges brought by AI require the collective response of the humanity, and that countries, when discussing and exploring future international norms governing AI, may proceed from the vision of building a community with a shared future for all mankind, as well as the concept of common security.

Published date: 2019. 11. 2

[INTERVIEW]

Korea-China relations are definitely entering a new phase of takeoff

With Qiu Guohong, Chinese Ambassador to Korea.

By Jaeho Hwang

Ambassador Qiu Guohong was born in Shanghai and graduated from the Shanghai International Studies University (SISU). He joined the Foreign Ministry in 1981 and previously served as ambassador to Nepal and director of security affairs. He is the longest-serving ambassador to Korea, after being appointed in February 2014. He is a fifth-tier master of baduk player and was second in a tournament hosted by the Chinese Ministry of Foreign Affairs.

It is said that public diplomacy has been the most active since Ambassador Qiu took office and, particularly, communication with experts in Korea has been the most frequent. Ahead of the trilateral summit among South Korea, China, and Japan in December, I met Ambassador Qiu at the embassy's reception room in Myeong-dong on Nov. 20 to discuss several pending issues between Korea and China.

Q. On October 1, China held a ceremony to celebrate the 70th anniver-

sary of its founding, at Tiananmen Square in Beijing. What impression did you get from the celebration?

A. As General Secretary Xi Jinping pointed out, the celebration of the 70th anniversary of the founding of "New China" was a grand feast under the backdrop of the "Great revolution that could happen once a hundred years", which the current world is facing. Through this, the People's Republic of China informed the world that it is not only still standing tall in the Eastern world, but also developing in a healthier way.

Greeting the 70th anniversary, the New China has made a huge achievement, which is recognized by the world. The fundamental reason why China was able to succeed was that it chose the proper method that conforms to state affairs. It is "socialism with Chinese characteristics". China will endeavor harder to realize its "The Centenaries' goal" and build a "rich, democratic, civilized, harmonious and beautiful socialist modernization state".

Q. China recently held the Fourth Plenary Session of the 19th Central Committee of the Communist Party of China. What was the main content of the session?

A. The session was held in Beijing from Oct. 28 to 31, 2019, and Xi Jinping delivered an important speech. The session reviewed and adopted the CPC Central Committee's decision on some major issues concerning how to uphold and improve the system of socialism with Chinese characteristics and advance the modernization of China's system and capacity for governance. This points a clear direction for each sector of China's internal and external construction.

The session also touched on China's diplomacy. China will maintain its independent, peaceful foreign policy, as well as making it more concrete while enhancing "the community of a shared future for mankind". China will first highly value peace, development, cooperation and co-prosperity, secondly, defend sovereignty, security and development interests steadily, and thirdly, safeguard world peace and promote joint development.

Q. Where are further Chinese domestic and foreign policies heading?

A. China is still a developing country and GDP per capita is falling behind in world rankings. Domestic economic development still has room for enhancement and regional imbalances are also serious. Therefore, economic development is still the priority goal for us to value for a long period of time. In terms of foreign policy, China aims to build a "new type of international relationship" and "a community of shared future for mankind".

China will maintain its diplomatic ideology of "building friendship and partnerships with neighboring countries" in the surrounding region significantly. China will continue to defend its legitimate rights and interests, but will not seek its own development at the cost of sacrificing the interests of other countries.

Q. China is currently carrying out its "Belt & Road Initiative (BRI)" strategy. How do you assess the performance of BRI and its following challenges?

A. BRI is an initiative for international economic cooperation. It is to find new growth engines for global economic development by using omnidirectional links and communication among countries, based on the foundation of infrastructure construction. Through such cooperation, we will build a new stage of cooperation in the international economy. However, BRI is clearly a new concept that has only just begun.

Therefore, it is understandable that still many countries doubt, have concerns, and even misunderstand the idea of BRI. Nonetheless, we believe that these problems and challenges will be solved naturally if the BRI construction projects continue to be pushed forward and show tangible results.

Q. Korea is concerned about the trade war between China and the U.S. What do you think about Koreans' concern?

A. There is actually no winner in the trade war. Both the U.S. and China will have a severe shock to their interests, but it will also have a negative impact on other countries, including South Korea. China does not want a trade war, but at the same time is not afraid of it. The door to negotiations is still wide open. We are trying to resolve this economic conflict through dialogue and negotiations with the U.S. China's attitude toward the trade war is to deal with its own affairs first.

China will continue to carry out higher levels of reform without wavering and will expand the scale of its opening. At the same time, China's huge domestic market will open wide to the world. China will continue to prepare for external environmental uncertainties with a firm policy of expanding the scale of its opening and will provide China's wisdom and measures to safeguard free trade and establish a more open global economic system.

Q. Is there any change in China's position on North Korea's nuclear weapons and the Korean Peninsula? Will it still carry out the U.N. Security Council resolutions?

A. China's position on the Korean Peninsula, including North Korea's nuclear weapons program, is very clear and consistent. China supports the denuclearization of the Korean Peninsula, supports peace and stability on the Korean Peninsula, and supports resolving the issues through dialogue and negotiations.

The fundamental contradiction on the Korean Peninsula is a security issue and the reason why it is difficult to resolve is due to the lack of trust among the concerned countries. We claim that the concerned countries should move forward in the same direction, strengthening dialogue and negotiations in a way to "keep the peace, step by step" in accordance with the "double-track".

At the same time, we must actively seek realistic ways to realize the complete denuclearization of the Korean Peninsula and a peace regime, and in the process, the reasonable concerns of the respective countries should be respected as well. As a permanent member of the Security Council and a responsible great member of the international community, China will faithfully implement the U.N. Security Council's resolution on North Korea. However, if North Korea complies with and implements the UNSC resolution, the international community also needs to ease its economic sanctions to some extent.

Q. How do you assess the current Korea-China relationship?

A. Since the establishment of diplomatic ties in 1992, Seoul and Beijing have gradually taken three steps: "cooperative partnership toward the 21st century", "fully cooperative partnership" and "strategic cooperative partnership". South Korea is China's third-largest trade partner, the largest importer and third-largest exporter. Human exchanges between the two countries have already surpassed the 10 million people.

The number of students studying abroad in each country is also the most in the world. Although we cannot deny that there is a contradiction between Korea and China, we have resolved tentative contradictions such as the THAAD issue, and the current relations between the two countries have returned to the right orbit. China will hold hands with South Korea to move forward and seek to create a more beautiful future for bilateral relations through communication and cooperation.

Q. Korea is looking forward to Xi Jinping's visit. When do you expect his visit to Korea will be realized?

A. President Moon Jae-in has already invited Xi Jinping several times.

And he has also accepted the invitation. However, we are only waiting for the right time and we are working on it. I and the Chinese Embassy in Seoul also hope that Xi Jinping's visit to Seoul will take place soon. For now, we can expect fruitful results from the Korea-China Summit, which will be held during the Korea-China-Japan Summit in mid-December.

Published date: 2019. 11. 30

1. 2. China and the World

[VIEW]

Managing the Fundamental Change of a Century in World Politics

By You Ji, Professor, University of Macau.

In recent years Chinese leader Xi Jinping has coined a widely used phrase "the fundamental change in world politics of the century" to portray the China's deteriorating external environment. Without giving a specific definition of what the change is, the general understanding is that it refers to the worsening Sino-U.S. relations in the advent of Washington finally coming up a strategic depiction on China as its peer adversary.

As a result the White house's has undergone a substantial break of its past China policy in way of conditional engagement. Increasingly, America is adopting a containment-oriented approach towards China's rise in the process of power transition. Interestingly U.S. vice president Pence denied that Washington opts for a new containment strategy against China in his October speech in the Wilson Centre. To many international analysts, however, the U.S. containment can be construed as both a selective one reflected by the decoupling effects of the on-going Sino-US trade, and as a targeted one, as reflected by U.S. military actions to push back the Chinese actions in the China Seas. Apparently China is probably under the heaviest international pressure since its opening to the outside world.

Beijing has adopted effective countermeasures to cope with U.S. offensive, effective in a sense that it has reaped visible gains in its periphery. Among them the most prominent foreign policy achievement for Beijing is the calm-down of Korean crisis with a number of shining summit meetings among four players, Seoul, Pyongyang, Washington and Beijing. Although all of them have gained one way or another in the rapprochement, Beijing has at least somewhat relieved from an imminent crisis that Hu Jintao once described as more serious than Taiwan's challenge.

President Xi Jinping should be congratulated for his great efforts in changing Kim Jong-un's basic stance on a number of key issues both inside the DPRK and towards the international security. To be more specific, three are worth mentioning. The first one is about convincing Kim Jong-un that a nuclear option is not an ideal one for guaranteeing the DPRK's survival as Pyongyang used to believe so. This paved the way for Kim Jong-un to reach a final decision to denuclearize, to the relief of all in the Peninsula and beyond. Secondly, in association with the first, Xi Jinping has successfully persuaded Kim Jong-un that economic development is the most effective means of regime survival in general and for Kim to consolidate legitimacy to rule in particular. Thirdly, Xi Jinping assured Kim Jong-un that it is possible for Pyongyang to improve relations with Washington, its long cherished foreign policy dream, and with Seoul once denuclearization is initiated, starting from freezing nuclear and long-range missile tests.

The beginning of the DPRK's denuclearization has proved the value of Xi's

Peninsula policy that differed his predecessor's. Simply put, Xi reordered China's priority sequence in pursuing crisis management in the Peninsula, from targeting stability as the top policy goal, followed by denuclearization to one that reversed this order. To Xi he rightly concluded that without denuclearization there was no stability to talk about. Then to achieve this end Xi maximized pressure on Pyongyang to yield to international pressure, through a sanction regime. Here he again changed the way that sanctions were conducted by his predecessor, which was largely symbolic. Instead Xi imposed substantial sanctions that not only hurt North Korea's economy but more critically its military readiness, e.g., through greatly reducing oil exportation, including the aviation fuel. Xi risked a complete break-down of the relationship and created a deadly enemy on its northern border but eventually he won the gamble, as Kim Jong-un blinked.

However, Xi Jinping's success in changing the course of development of North Korea is not cost free. Beijing's resumption of large amount of aid to an unpredictable government may not bear fruit if Kim Jong-un eventually eats his words on denuclearization, which is possible due to other factors beyond his control, such as continued U.S. hostility or a change of government in Seoul. Today China has to shoulder more responsibilities of security guarantee for North Korea in the absence of U.S. assurance in this regard. Four bilateral summit meetings in a short span of less than a year were really abnormal for two countries just recovering from the worst shape in the bilateral relationship. It may not be wise that Beijing has so quickly discarded its earlier depiction of North Korea as a normal neighbor, not a traditional ally. A Kim Jong-un trap is always possible for Beijing to handle, given that denuclearization is on pause today, and may be delayed for a long time to come. Then a success may turn into a nightmare.

In the last few years also Beijing has consolidated its regional standing vis-a-vis the U.S., taking advantage of the latter's unilateralism that alienated its allies and partners through trade tariff sanctions, unreasonable demands for more payment for U.S. soldiers deployed in the allied countries and poisoned personal ties with regional leaders. First, China has improved relations with Japan, realizing a state visit by the Japanese Prime Minister in 2018. Xi's state visit to Japan in April 2020 has been set with a return tour by Japan's Emperor in planning. Such a frequency of summit visits is in sharp contrast to the fact that the two countries had not had any state visits for almost seven years. In a way the improvement has come up relatively easily, as Xi decided to lower the tension caused by the Daiyus/Senkakus dispute and moved the bilateral relations forward, diluting the negativity of the unpleasant history.

Secondly, China has too improved the relations with India. The Sino-Indian Doklam confrontation in 2017 almost got the two countries in a sizeable war. Both of them then realized that a sense relationship between them got them nowhere in the current complicated world politics. In 2018 and again in 2019 two summit meetings were successfully conducted between Xi and Modi in Wuhan and in Chennai. Through a heart-to-heart exchange of views they finally set the agreements on dos and don'ts so that the bilateral ties have become stabilized to the benefits of both.

Finally, Beijing has made the move to improve relations with ASEAN with a good outcome. What Beijing has done is also simple: to end a cycle of assertiveness over the disputes in the South China Sea, which is relatively calm among the disputants, although tension remains high between the Chinese and American navies there. Yet the latter is not about the territorial disputes any more but over geo-strategic rivalry. Today Sino-ASEAN interaction is mostly in a positive area to the relief of Beijing. A stable relationship with ASEAN ensures stability in China's backyard and allows Beijing to concentrate on U.S. pressure.

Yet there is a big question mark about China's overall standing in the "change of a century in world politics". Probably the accumulated positive effects of China improving ties with its immediate neighbors cannot offset the negative impact of worsening Sino-U.S. relations. China's external environment will remain precarious as long as its relations with Washington do not improve.

Published date: 2019. 11. 09

[REVIEW]

Unexpected Achievements with Emerging Challenges on Sixth Anniversary of BRI

By Xue Li, Senior Fellow of
Chinese Academy of Social Sciences.

It has been six years since the Belt and Road Initiative (BRI), regarded as a Century Project, was proposed in 2013. BRI is now exerting an increasingly significant effect on the whole world when influencing China itself greatly. Overall, positive opinions of the many from both home and abroad coexist with some doubts of the few. The researches done over the past six years offer the author the following judgments.

At first, BRI was mainly aimed at promoting cooperation with developing countries and then it gradually integrated cooperation with developed countries into its framework. It is implemented by means of memorandums of understanding, the third-party market cooperation, small multilateral mechanisms, resolutions of international organizations and the like. Building BRI jointly is both a means of deepening economic cooperation and an important way to improve the global development mode and reform global governance system. Internally, BRI will support to realize the Chinese Dream and externally, it serves to build a Community with a Shared Future for Mankind. It demonstrates China's foreign policy concept such as Non-alignment Policy and Partnership Diplomacy. Meanwhile, it embodies China's independent foreign policy of peace it pursued consistently. BRI has been divided into different levels. First of all, it is the top-level designing for China's diplomacy under Xi Administration; secondly, it is the guideline of China's diplomacy in Xi's period; thirdly, it is the way for China to carry out global governance; fourth, it serves as the main platform for China to provide public goods for the world, etc.

China has signed 195 documents with 136 countries and 30 international organizations under the framework of BRI. A large number of international organizations, including UN, have passed resolutions to extend their endorsement of BRI. What's more, some countries consider it as a great opportunity to promote self-development. After gradually changing their attitudes to BRI, some developed countries finally participated in the construction of it by way of the third-party market cooperation. While criticizing BRI, some developed countries also began to borrow ideas from BRI.

For China, BRI, can achieve several goals in a way the host countries can accept, which is to strengthen their bilateral relations, to stretch China's national interests and to assume more responsibilities as a major power.

The achievements BRI made is far beyond people's expectations. Meanwhile, BRI itself also needs to grow with a constant adjustment and enrichment, and this is in accordance with China's concept and style of world governance. The accomplishments achieved by reform and opening-up prove that the strategy-groping forward after deciding the general direction works well.

These challenges consist of three aspects as below. As a developing country and late comer of the nation state system, China still confronts a series of challenges, namely, to further develop itself, to assume more responsibilities as a major power, to keep the sustainability of BRI construction. In host countries, these challenges include their concerns over China's increasing influence, their political unrest, the common's misunderstandings of some projects and the so-called debt trap fabricated by Western media, etc.

Some developed countries and developing powers are worried that their interests and sphere of influence would be affected by China's rise and thus throw doubts on the intentions of BRI. What's worse, the sole superpower, the US, sees China as its strategic competitor and even balances and oppresses China with the Indo-Pacific Rebalance Strategy and trade war.

As a Century Project mentioned by Xi Jinping, the success of BRI relies on its long-term effects rather than its short term outcomes. Consequently, these challenges must be tackled well to achieve the sustainability of BRI. To ensure that goal, China needs to take the following measures at least.

Firstly, strengthen the management of BRI. More priority should be assigned to the quality of projects rather than its quantity when choosing projects. When cooperating with some countries on some certain projects, China had better slow down and even suspend them. Some projects of high risks can be carried out after conditions allow.

Secondly, reduce the doubts of host countries and gain further understanding and support. Thus the cooperation pattern needs to be formed where the host countries take a major role and China, holding its veto power, plays a complementary role. China should show more respect for the host countries in terms of way and speed of construction.

Thirdly, China should regard those developed countries who are willing to cooperate as important partners when promoting BRI. China also needs to strengthen the mechanism of bilateral cooperation and determine the region the host countries and the projects for the third-party market cooperation, for instance, China and South Korea may choose country A while China and Japan have country B.

Some developed countries and developing powers express no willingness to support BRI openly. In this regard, China needs to be patient. Expanding the circle of friends in various manners is part of building BRI against the background that the competition between China and the US is increasingly fierce and will be prolonged. China's concept of pursuing cooperation and mutual benefits with openness will gain acknowledgement from more and more countries.

China needs to realize it clearly that qualitatively, the essence of Sino-US relations remains the same and the United States is China's competitor rather than its enemy. Therefore, "Decoupling" and "Comprehensive confrontation" are not within options. However, wrestling with it is a better alternative. That is to say, China should strengthen its relationship with Americans who are still willing to cooperate with China. By doing so, China may continue to use the comparative advantages in science and technology, capital, market, education, and other aspects.

Briefly, with its impressive achievements, BRI is likely to become one of the foreign policy decisions that influence the world most since 1949. In the meantime, the challenges facing it are increasingly protruding. It is normal for a project lasting for about one hundred years. To build BRI in a sustainable way, China needs to maintain concentration and keep patient when tackling challenges. (Liu He, from the China Foreign Affairs University, assisted with this article.)

Published date: 2019. 11. 16

[VIEW]

China and the US should make a strategic compromise

By Li Kaisheng, Research Fellow, Shanghai Academy of Social Sciences.

Unfortunately, while most East Asian countries enjoy economic prosperity, the whole region has lived in the shadow of a fragmented security order. Yes, there are some security arrangements, such as the U.S.-led bilateral alliances and ASEAN Regional Forum, but these mechanisms either only protect the limited members or have no muscle to manage regional challenges.

So how do you build an inclusive and effective regional security institution? In international politics, institutions usually originate from the need to resolve certain problems. But the different security challenges may have varying possibilities in breeding and establishing an institution. In East Asia, which security issue will create a security institution? The answer may be the Korean nuclear issue.

Why? It is because that, compared with other security challenges in East Asia, the Korean nuclear issue has the following characteristics.

Firstly, the issue covers the main East Asia players: China, the U.S., Russia, Japan and the two Koreas. If it succeeds, an institution based on the Korean nuclear issue would be a very representative and inclusive arrangement. Any East Asia security mechanism should especially include China and the U.S. But with the South China Sea, Taiwan and Diaoyu issues, the U.S. isn't recognized by China as a direct concerned party, thus it would be impossible to construct an inclusive institution based on these issues.

Secondly, in the Korean nuclear issue, most parties share the common important interest of denuclearization. Even North Korea now shows it is willing to give up its nuclear plans if certain requirements are satisfied. The sharing interest is a precondition to create a security arrangement. Relatively, there is less overlap of interest among the concerned parties in other East Asia security challenges.

Lastly, the Korean nuclear issue is tied to a series of security challenges, such as how to end the Korean War, normalization of North Korea's relations with a few powers, and the future of the U.S.-South Korea alliance, etc. Fundamentally, these issues should be solved together by a comprehensive arrangement or it is impossible for North Korea to give up its nuclear plans.

Of course, it is not an easy task to create a new security arrangement. When the six-party talks achieved progress, some policymakers and researchers believed a new security institution would come into being. But so far nothing has happened. Here, some lessons should be learned and remembered.

The most important lesson is always to consider denuclearization as the highest interest. The failure of the six-party talks was in large part the consequence of strategic ignorance of the previous American administrations. During the George W. Bush administration, the Afghanistan War and Iraq War were considered as its priorities; not enough resolve and time were poured into the Korea nuclear issue. The Obama administration insisted on the so-called strategic patience policy, thus fewer initiatives were taken on the Korean Peninsula.

Therefore, to maintain the current dynamics of solving the nuclear issue, one of preconditions is that the U.S. doesn't shift its focus from the Korean nuclear issue again. Moreover, to achieve the international cooperation that is the key to denuclearization, the U.S. should stop poisoning its relations with China by ending the trade war.

Fundamentally, the U.S. should be ready for a new institution on the Korean Peninsula. If there is no peace regime, it is hard to expect that North Korea would give up its nuclear plans. America has considered its bilateral alliance with South Korea as one of the pillars of its hegemony in East Asia. But for solving the Korean nuclear issue, the South Korea-U.S. alliance may be at least adjusted to some degree. Given that to balance China's rise is one of the potential goals for this alliance, the U.S. is obviously not ready to give up this comfortable tool.

Thus, to create a new security institution, China and the U.S. should make a strategic compromise in achieving peaceful co-existence and competition in East Asia. When there is rising tension between two powers, it is not easy to achieve. But in the long-term, even though competition may be inevitable between the established and rising powers, this competition should be based on the rules and managed by some mechanisms.

It should be noted that in the process of compromising the two powers and establishing the new security institution, South Korea may play a more active and positive role. South Korea is an ally of the U.S. and friend of China. When strategic distrust is still rooted deeply between two giants, the neutral initiative from South Korea would be more welcomed in regional-order planning.

All these efforts should be aimed at denuclearization and establishing a new security institution in East Asia. Since the 1990s, although the Korean nuclear issue has been a challenge to regional stability and frustrated the concerned parties so many times, we have to consider it as an opportunity for building a lasting peace in East Asia.

Published date: 2018. 09. 15

[VIEW]

China-U.S. trade negotiations: Need to persevere until impending end

By Yu Donghui, Chief U.S. Correspondent,
China Review News Agency.

Between late April and early May, the U.S. and China are pushing forward with trade negotiations, hoping to ratify the final treaty before a bilateral summit between their heads of state. After initial progress in April, President Donald Trump said we would see a conclusion of negotiations in four weeks. Along with this statement, the China-U.S. trade deal is approaching its final stages after a turbulent path. Now it is time to end the Sino-American trade war that has lasted a year.

As Trump put it, "A lot of really good things have been negotiated and agreed to, and the U.S. and China had agreed on a lot of the most difficult points" in trade negotiations. From his statement, we can see that the impending deal will be "Very comprehensive" and "Topical". Also, Trump recently announced President Xi Jinping's White House visit, illustrating Trump's will to conclude the deal with China as soon as possible. With the 2020 U.S. presidential election approaching, Trump needs to revitalize his reputation by bringing "The grand victory" to his people, especially when the American economy and stock market have not been strong, as expected a few months ago. Since his escape from investigation over the "Russian scandal", there has been a big increase in the possibility that Trump will again run for the Oval Office, without any risk of impeachment.

The Sino-American negotiations have provided him with a more predictable environment and China, in its turn, now has a motive to maintain a good relationship with Trump, who has a greater chance of winning another four-year term.

The Chinese economy needs to pursue a continuous and stable development trajectory through advanced promises on reforming and opening, as well as enacting those promises. It has been reported that China promised to resolve the U.S. trade imbalance issue with a sizeable purchase

in the next six years and to secure a concrete reform procedure in terms of intellectual property and technological transfer in accordance with the "Structural reform" that the U.S. focuses on.

Even though Trump still faces domestic hard-liners' pressure not to accept any "Weak" deals, there is a consensus that the negotiation needs to be concluded as swiftly as possible with a deal both parties can accept. The biggest obstacle remaining is whether the U.S. will maintain tariffs on Chinese goods worth $250 billion to utilize the measure as a one-sided "Tool of legal enforcement". If the U.S. were to maintain this particular clause and use it as a sanction if China failed to comply with the agreement, this approach will not sit well with the Chinese who will deem it as an "Unfair agreement". If the tariffs persist, it implies that the trade war is not over and could intensify.

Last year proved that the trade war is hurting both parties. In 2018, American exports grew 7 per cent worldwide while Chinese exports shrank 7 per cent. During the first two months of 2019, Chinese exports to the U.S. decreased 20 per cent. The International Monetary Fund (IMF) warns that American efforts to decrease its trade deficit with China by imposing tariffs before the trade negotiations are doomed to fail. The latest IMF report argues that imposing 25 per cent tariffs on Chinese goods to the U.S. amounts to $540 billion annually, and Chinese retaliation tariffs worth $120 billion on American goods negatively impact American gross domestic product (GDP) by 0.3 to 0.6 per cent while decreasing Chinese GDP by 0.5 to 1.5 per cent.

Trump has hoped for the return of manufacturing industry to the U.S. and an influx of foreign investment, as well as the creation of American jobs. However, the China-U.S. trade war has affected the American investment environment and, in the current era of highly globalized industries, it discourages Chinese businesses from investing in the U.S. and harms international enterprises linked to China in terms of manufacturing.

According to a U.S. survey, the American trade deficit with China reached its highest of $419 billion. The resolution of the deficit through a trade war has not panned out as Trump hoped. Now he is faced with the pressure of a new election after the successful implementation of his campaign promises. Even if there were to be an “Incomplete deal”, as many American experts predict, there exists a reason to end a trade war that benefits nobody.

Of course, Trump’s fickleness faces pressure from hard-liners on China and there are geopolitical, strategic and competitive elements to consider before ratifying the deal between the U.S. and China, making it hard to call the deal a success.

White House trade adviser and hard-liner Peter Navarro cited his Chinese negotiation counterpart, saying “The last mile of the marathon is actually the longest and the hardest”. It is still indeed questionable whether Sino-American strategic competition will ease even after negotiations end.

Published date: 2019. 05. 11

1. 3. China and the Korean Peninsula

[VIEW]

North Korea and the new cooperation mechanism in Northeast Asia

By Li Chengri, Research Fellow, Chinese Academy of Social Sciences.

In the year 2017, war tension on in the Korean Peninsula left Northeast Asia in dangerous place. However, in 2018 drastic changes are taking place faster than expected. The changes taking place in North Korea are truly remarkable.

First of all, North Korea clearly declared the transition from Byungjin Line (parallel development of nuclear and economic construction) to concentration on economic development. Secondly, North Korea' leader Kim Jong-un several times mentioned the denuclearization of the Korean Peninsula. In particular, he directly agreed with President Moon Jae-In about creating a Korean Peninsula free of nuclear weapons and nuclear threats.

The estranged relationship between North Korea and China due to nuclear issues, and the deteriorating inter-Korean relations were prominently improved and led to the first-ever U.S.-North Korean summit. In addition, North Korea's policy decisions have been made public in several reports. This implies fundamental changes in politics, economy, social, and foreign relations.

Kim Jong-un's visit to Russia and a summit with Japan's Prime Minister Abe are planned, and the second U.S.-North Korean Summit will be a turning point for the changes on the Korean Peninsula. This change began from North Korea and is having a huge impact on the Korean Peninsula, moreover, even to the dynamics in Northeast Asia. North Korea is the only undeveloped area in Northeast Asia. Although North Korea has proposed intensive economic construction projects and is pushing for national development by presenting a "Five-year Strategy", it will be difficult to achieve visible results within a short time without fundamental improvement of the surrounding environment.

The infrastructure situation in North Korea is relatively poor. Without fundamental improvement, it is difficult to get full-fledged investment from outside the country. Under the current situation, massive modifications and investment should be made to the North's infrastructure — railroads, roads and power. Because infrastructure investment is large and has a long payback period, infrastructure investments must be guaranteed by the relevant countries or be funded by international financial institutions.

In addition, the international community's cooperation or cooperation system is highly desirable, as most investment or development in North Korea is difficult for any single country to handle alone. In particular, the cooperation and efforts of Korea, China, and Japan are essential.

The only cooperation system functioning in Northeast Asia involves Korea, China, and Japan. There are many new ideas about North Korean regional development, but the most realistic is a trilateral cooperation mechanism. To establish North Korea's trust in the international community, it is now necessary for trilateral cooperation to work strategically on developing North Korea, which is the biggest issue in Northeast Asia.

First, we must support and cooperate with North Korea's changes. For North Korea, it is never an easy decision to switch toward denuclearization or economic construction. In other words, successful economic construction is critical to Kim Jong-un as a historical sense of duty and involving great risk. If by any chance North Korea fails to achieve positive results, it could have a huge negative impact not only on North Korea but also on the Korean Peninsula. Therefore, it is necessary to approach North Korea's new national development on economic construction concentration in terms of peace and development on the Korean Peninsula and in Northeast Asia.

Second, support for construction of the North Korean economy should not be carried out independently by China, South Korea, or Japan, but rather at the level of economic integration in Northeast Asia. North Korea for its part will thus not rely on a particular country to receive abundant resources for development but make efforts to maintain some degree of balance. The construction of infrastructure such as electric power, roads, and railroads necessary for economic reconstruction will also be difficult for the country on its own. Therefore, China, South Korea, and Japan should form an economic cooperation mechanism.

Third, strategic thinking and approach to the new changes in North Korea should be attempted. Currently, it is necessary to invite North Korea or Mongolia to join the trilateral cooperation mechanism. If this is not feasible, at least North Korea should be accepted as an observer so we can provide an environment that lets North Korea establish an identity as a part of Northeast Asia. The situation in Northeast Asia cannot and should never be reversed. For more than 70 years after World War II, the Korean Peninsula has been divided. Now, the people of both Koreas and even Northeast Asia are wishing for peace on the Korean Peninsula and for regional prosperity.

This is the public sentiment in this region and it cannot be stopped by any greater power or game theories. The three countries should altogether contribute to the prosperity and cooperation system of Northeast Asia by fully understanding the historical trends and supporting North Korean economic development through government-led, infrastructure building and multilateral means.

Published date: 2018. 12. 15

[VIEW]

Xi's visit to two Koreas will contribute to building peace on Korean Peninsula

By Kwok Waifung, President, China Review News Agency, Hong Kong.

If Xi Jinping's visit to South and North Korea works out smoothly this year, there must be more dynamic changes between China-North Korea or in promoting peace on the Korean Peninsula.

North Korea's supreme leader Kim Jong-un asked Xi for a visit quite a while ago. On Jan. 10, Chinese spokesman Lu Kang said, "Elites (high-ranking officials) of China and North Korea have a long tradition of mutual visits; this exchange has been the major engine for the development of China-DPRK relations. We are further going to strengthen this interaction, strategically deepen the communication, and expand the exchanges and cooperation. Regarding the updated issues on this, we will announce them to the public".

From Lu Kang's statement, we can predict that Xi will definitely visit North Korea this year and the schedule is the only matter to be worked out, nothing else. If Xi's visit comes true, it will be his first visit to North

Korea since he became president. It has been 14 years since a Chinese president visited North Korea — that was Hu Jintao in 2005. Looking back, we can see how China-North Korea relations have fluctuated.

We saw Xi and Kim's summit in Beijing on Jan. 8. This can be interpreted as Xi's positive intention to visit North Korea this year. First, corresponding to China-North Korea's historical change, this relationship has to be improved to a more concrete level. 1) Especially, this year is the 70th anniversary of China-North Korea diplomatic relations; therefore, it is meaningful to celebrate this as a historical point for a sustainable march forward. 2) Since last year, China and North Korea have been moving forward; for instance, they maintained mutual exchanges in high-ranking officials, strengthened strategic talks, and held amicable interchanges to foster healthier, long-term development.

Second, corresponding to peace on the Korean Peninsula, China should promote its "Four Supports" on the Korean Peninsula situation. 1) Support North Korea's sustainable position on a denuclearized Korean Peninsula, 2) Support the sustainable improvement of inter-Korean relations, 3) Support the opening and outcome of the U.S.-North Korean Summit, 4) Support rationally solving each party's interest through dialogue. In other words, Xi's fundamental aim in visiting North Korea is not limited just to China-North Korean relations; it should play a bigger role for the Korean Peninsula's peace and prosperity. From the above two perspectives, Xi's visit is significantly necessary.

What we have to look at here is that Xi talked with President Moon Jae-in at the APEC meeting in Papua New Guinea last November. Back then,

Moon invited Xi to visit South Korea as soon as possible and Xi replied that he would do so the next year at an appropriate time.

Again, this means there is a high possibility that Xi will visit both Koreas this year. From the geographical aspect, China's influence on the Korean Peninsula can never be underestimated; as well as the Korean Peninsula's influence on China. The world will pay attention to the great strategic meanings and value of Xi's visit to both Koreas.

Xi has many times referred to building a community with a shared future for mankind and Asia. Now, any major changes in Chinese policy for the Korean Peninsula largely depend on changes in Xi's thoughts and ideologies. For example, Xi believes in: "Settle the dispute with conversation, narrow down the differences with negotiation". As the most important principle in dealing with Korean Peninsula issues.

When two Koreas were close to war Xi kept talking with the U.S., South and North Korea, and Russia, sticking to the principle of communication, and eventually eased the risk of war. Everyone might already know that Xi's enlightened awareness, as well as his effort to overcome the difficulties, has finally improved East Asia's security.

Xi has suggested building the Community of Shared Destiny of Mankind and the Community of Common Destiny of Asia. Here, the top priority is to build a new value not only within East Asia but in the world. This value represents something more than a normal ideology; aiming to drive East Asia without any collisions or resistance, building the "Peace, Development, Cooperation, and Common" era, and aiming for a new form of international relations where common benefit can be created through cooperation. This peaceful green international development strategy aims for a broader international norm. This definitely is the new direction for East Asia's security.

Concluding, Xi's visit to both Koreas this year will contribute to building peace on the Korean Peninsula. We can look forward to seeing how this will lead to settling disputes across the whole of East Asia, to the benefit of future generations.

Published date: 2019. 03. 02

[INTERVIEW]

How China looks at the Inter-Korean Summit

With Fan Gaoyue, Guest Professor, Sichuan University.
By Jaeho Hwang

The inter-Korean summit on April 27 left a deeply moving impression. South Korean President Moon Jae-in and North Korean leader Kim Jong-un had a historical moment at Panmunjeom, crossing the border to each other's country holding hands. Watching them walking together and sharing a big hug was barely imaginable after the Korean Peninsula recently seemed just one step from war. Furthermore, the Panmunjeom Declaration is de facto the declaration of the end of war between the North and South. In other words, the neighboring states of the Korean Peninsula should also prepare to greet a new security environment.

China, as an old external power of Korea, seems to be considering its own interest from various angles as well as congratulating on the well-done summit. In this sense, I've held an email interview with Gaoyue Fan, an authoritative Chinese militarist. Gaoyue Fan, a retired senior colonel, is now a guest professor at the Collaborative Innovation Center for Security and Development of Western Frontier China, Sichuan University. He was director of the U.S. and Europe Military Research Office at the PLA Academy of Military Science (AMS) in Beijing. His research interests include U.S. military affairs, international security and cooperation, international arms control and disarmament.

Q. What do you think of the North/South Korean summit?

A. I think the North/South Korean summit was a great success because (1) Kim Jong-un was the first North Korean leader to step on South Korean soil in 65 years; (2) the atmosphere of the summit was friendly, sincere and harmonious; (3) the summit resulted in a joint declaration which is welcomed by both Koreas and the international community; (4) the summit has relaxed tense situations on the Korean Peninsula and improved the North-South Korea relations.

Q. How do you assess the achievements of the North/South Korean summit?

A. The achievements are enormous and mainly embodied in the "Panmunjeom Declaration for Peace, Prosperity and Unification of the Korean Peninsula", which includes three aspects and 13 articles. The most important messages are that South and North Korea will reconnect the blood relations of the people and bring forward the future of co-prosperity and unification, will make joint efforts to alleviate the acute military tension and practically eliminate the danger of war on the Korean Peninsula and confirmed the common goal of realizing, through complete denuclearization, a nuclear-free Korean Peninsula. The international community is pleased to hear these messages and hopes all these will come true.

Q. Would you please tell me how you envision North-South Korea relations after the summit?

A. I guess North and South Korea will not take the paths they took after the North/South Korean summits in 2000 and 2007, and will adopt some concrete measures to improve their relations. First, they will reduce hostile activities along the 38th parallel; second, they will increase communications with each other to avoid misunderstanding and misperceptions; third, South Korea might send some humanitarian aid to North Korea to help its people out of the current plight; fourth, North Korea will cease its military provocations either on land, in the air or on the sea; fifth, North and South Korea will coordinate their efforts in denuclearization of the peninsula and replace the armistice agreement with a peace treaty.

Q. Would you please let me know how you look at future North Korea-U.S. relations?

A. As you know, North Korean leader Kim Jong-un is going to meet U.S. President Donald Trump in late May or early June. And Trump twitted his welcome and support for the North/South Korean summit. I think the result of the summit has met U.S. expectations by agreeing to work for the "Complete denuclearization of the Korean Peninsula" and establish "Permanent" and "Solid" peace on the peninsula, and has laid a good foundation for the coming Kim-Trump summit. Therefore, North Korea-U.S. relations are going to improve if North Korea does not break its word.

Q. Mr. Fan, what are the implications of the North/South Korean summit for China?

A. As you know, North Korean leader Kim Jong-un paid an informal visit to China before he met President Moon Jae-in. China supported and encouraged the North/South Korean summit and was happy to see its fruitful results. China has long been advocating that North Korean nuclear and security issues should be solved peacefully through dialogue and negotiations. China hosted the six-party talks for years and adheres to the "Dual track approach" in dealing with the North Korean nuclear issue; that is, to advance denuclearization and peace-building at the same time leading ultimately to the replacement of the armistice agreement with a peace treaty. The Panmunjeom Declaration shows that North and South Korea are moving in the right direction. It is a victory of the North/South Korean summit. It is also a victory of China's foreign policy.

However, it seems that North Korea and South Korea have devalued China's important role in denuclearizing North Korea and keeping peace, security and stability on the Korean Peninsula by saying that "South and North Korea agreed to actively pursue trilateral meetings involving the two Koreas and the United States, or quadrilateral meetings involving the two Koreas, the United States and China, with a view to declaring an end to the war, turning the armistice into a peace treaty, and establishing a permanent and solid peace regime".

The quoted sentence implies that denuclearizing and peace-building on the Korean Peninsula has little to do with China and the two Koreas can do it with or without China. But the fact is that China is a neighboring country of the two Koreas and a signatory of the armistice agreement of the Korean War. Any nuclear test, nuclear weapon or armed conflict on the Korean Peninsula will endanger China's national security interests and therefore have something to do with China. How could China be excluded from the denuclearization and peace-building of the Korean Peninsula? I wish North and South Korea could see this and try to get

China's whole-hearted support.

Q. Do you have any other comments on the summit?

A. There are people who hold negative views of the summit, suspecting whether North and South Korea would really execute the Panmunjeom Declaration just as they failed to carry out the Common Declaration of the North and South signed in 2000 and the Declaration on the Development of North-South Relations, Peace and Prosperity signed in 2007. But I think things might be different this time and I am optimistic about the implementation of the Panmunjeom Declaration.

The U.S.-North Korean summit is just around the corner; the only issues to be handled from now on are simply the place and date. No matter how, enormous change is approaching the Korean Peninsula. A delicate calculation of each state's interest is inevitable. However, the most significant challenge is to draw the solution minimizing the conflict of interests. Here, enhancing China's engagement as a supporter of the peace regime, not as the obstacle, is one of the critical missions Korea is facing.

Published date: 2018. 05. 05

[INTERVIEW]

Chinese reporter's views of Korea's security environment

With Guo Zhijun, Director, International News Department, China Review News Agency

By Jaeho Hwang

The 17th Shangri-la dialogue was held in Singapore early this month; the greatest diplomacy and security discussion banquet in terms of its volume and quality. More than 1,000 professionals, journalists and delegations consisting of heads of government, general staff and bureaucrats from about 40 countries attended.

Indian Prime Minister Narendra Modi delivered the keynote address and U.S. Defense Minister James Mattis continued the first session. Song Young-moo, the Korean Minister of Defense, also attended as part of the Korean delegation to discuss North Korea's denuclearization and inter-Korean relations. The Shangri-La Dialogue focuses on worldwide diplomacy and security issues.

This time more than 100 Chinese journalists attended. Watching them, I wondered what they thought about current issues. So I interviewed Ms. Zhijun Guo, on June 3, who has attended the dialogue for several years. It was a unique occasion with a professor interviewing a journalist.

Guo is a director of the China Review News Agency international news department. She focuses on interviews and East Asia security issues, especially peninsula issues and Sino-U.S. relations. She was a professional associate of Colombia University's Weatherhead East Asian Institute in New York City from 2015-2016. She also has a master's degree from the Bristol University and a master's degree from Hong Kong Baptist University.

Q. What is your feeling about the 17th Shangri-La Dialogue?

A. From my perspective, the Shangri-La Dialogue always gives me lots of opportunities to keep in touch with the latest news and ideas about Asia-Pacific security and cooperation among many countries. I always feel that the Shangri-La Dialogue is an open and free platform to listen and learn different views of security and defense policies between Western and Eastern countries. Although many concepts are not the same, the opportunities supported by the Shangri-La Dialogue are precious. As a journalist, I always feel lucky when I come to Singapore to do interviews at the Shangri-La Dialogue.

Q. What is the most impactful thing from your interviews?

A. I looked for several months to premier Modi's keynote speech at this year's Shangri-La Dialogue. I wanted to hear his views on the Indo-Pacific and if he would criticize China. In fact, unlike U.S. Secretary of Defense Mattis, his tone is gentle and he emphasizes the importance of relations between India and China. He said "A two-day informal summit with President Xi helped us cement our understanding that strong and stable relations between our two nations are an important factor for global peace and progress . . . Asia and the world will have a better future when India and China work together in trust and confidence". I think this is the most impactful thing I remember from this year's dialogue.

Q. How do you view about the Trump-Kim Summit which will be held next week in Singapore?

A. I am looking forward to this historic summit. I really hope the summit can be held successfully and achieve some real progress on North Korea denuclearization issue. This problem has threatened East Asia countries for more than 20 years. I believe no one in these countries want to see bombs and real 'fire'. North Korea leader and his team should think carefully that do they what to be a part of world or not? I hope the U.S, the DPRK and other related regional countries have wisdom to use this opportunity.

Q: What did you think about the inter-Korean summit in April this year?

A. I went to Seoul to cover the inter-Korean summit this April and I highly admire what President Moon did. In my opinion, President Moon Jae-in has consistently appealed for dialogue to defuse tensions surrounding the Korean Peninsula and held the summit with Kim Jong-un successfully on April 27. This summit is a symbol for opening a path toward peace on the peninsula. I have visited South Korea many times and I always like talking with my Korean friends. Just like the theme "Peace, a new start", I hope the peninsula can enjoy peace and prosperity forever.

Q. Can you compare cross-strait relations with the two Koreas?

A. This is really a hard question. To some extent, I don't think these two relations can be compared because of the different national context. However, cross-strait relations are sometimes similar relations macroscopically. Premier Li said "No matter how the situation on the island may evolve, the fraternal bond between the mainland and Taiwan will not be severed". I think there is a kind of similar brotherhood between the ROK and DPRK, although they are two different independent countries acknowledged by many nations. No matter how serious the situation, I believe both sides should communicate peacefully because we can only find a way out through dialogue.

Q. They were heavy questions, here is a light one: What is your impression of the Korean wave?

A. I love K-pop and Korean variety shows. I am a big fan of TVXQ and I learn Korean from Korean dramas. In my mind, many Korean variety shows are creative and funny, which make me laugh loudly. K-pop has a huge number of fans in China and I think some Chinese entertainment shows could learn from Korean cultural industries.

Q. Do you have any other comments?

A. I'd like to introduce my press. China Review News Agency (CRNA) is the first digital network news agency in the Greater China region, with its extensive news information-gathering networks in Taiwan, Hong Kong, China and the U.S. CRNA provides readers with around-the-clock coverage of important news, comments and in-depth analysis from the regions. On Jun. 3, 2005, CRNA published its first article via www.CRNTT.com, the official website of CRNA. CRNA also runs a monthly magazine, China Review, and a publishing house. Through its subsidiary, the China Review Think Tank Foundation, a cooperative network has been formed with more than 200 think tanks and 2000 experts around the globe.

As a professor, it was a very special and rare experience to cover a journalist's views and thoughts on recent dynamic Korean Peninsula diplomacy and the security environment. At the same time, it was a chance to hear how the Korean wave is still viewed on the mainland. We concluded our interview wishing Ms. Guo a bright and vibrant future. Maybe next time we meet, the journalist will interview the professor.

Published Date: 2018. 06. 16

Ⅰ China's Foreign Relations

1. 4. China and Neighbors

[REVIEW]

Japan and Korea's China dilemma: Dragon slayer vs Dragon hugger

By Jaeho Hwang, Professor, Hankuk University of Foreign Studies, Seoul.

The Korea-Japan Experts Seminar was held in Tokyo on August 27, when Korea-Japan relations were sharply conflicting.

The Center for Contemporary Korean Studies of the Institute of East Asian Studies from Keio University and the Global Security Cooperation Center from Hankuk University of Foreign Studies held talks with the theme of "Mutual Understanding of Korea-Japan Security Strategy", under the auspices of the Korea Foundation.

Two sessions were held with Center for Contemporary Korean Studies director Nishino Junya as a chairman. The first was "The strategy of Korea-Japan surrounding the situation on the Korean Peninsula" while the second was "Korea and Japan's response on the strategic competition between the U.S. and China". Researchers from both countries were basically aware of the insecurity and instability of the rapidly changing regional security order, however, they had some similarities as well as

differences in their response strategies.

In terms of North Korea policy, Korea and Japan differed most. On the other hand, Korea and Japan also focused on their relationship with China instead of the unilateral choice of the ROK-U.S. or U.S.-Japan alliance to secure their national interests. This seminar focused on the current security environment rather than the recent history issues. Summaries of experts from each two countries are as follows:

In the first session, Professor Koh Yoo-hwan from Dongguk University shared the reason why there is no progress in denuclearization of the Korean Peninsula over a year after the summit in Singapore. He said the cause comes from the mutual distrust that no one can confirm North Korea's complete denuclearization or its bright future. Once we enter the actual denuclearization stage, the issue of trust will become more serious. Maybe the North Korean nuclear issue is already in a difficult stage for scientific declaration and verification, he said. Therefore, once we decide to trust, we must rush with the freeze that will halt the nuclear missile program that is still in operation. Even in terms of the concept of denuclearization and a comprehensive agreement, the collective settlement to achieve denuclearization, which is very close to disarmament at once, may not be easy. As U.S. President Donald Trump said, both Koreas and the United States must find the common benefit in creating a roadmap of comprehensive agreements and phased implementation rather than being hasty.

The Vice Director of the Institute for National Security Strategy, Lee Ki-dong, said that even though North Korea has strict sanctions from the international community, rapidly changed its national policy from possessing nuclear power to denuclearization, or from dual policy of nuclear and economic development to an economic centralized policy, and remained in long-term stalemate with U.S. relations, there is no clear sign of instability. Economically, North Korea is pouring all its efforts into breaking through the sanctions by encouraging and mobilizing internal capabilities, with the emphasis on self-sufficiency, self-rehabilitation and conservation. Externally, it is seeking to resume negotiations on denuclearization based on trust between the leaders of the U.S. and North Korea, Lee said. The current speed of negotiations is still slow due to ROK-U.S. military exercises or military reinforcements. However, there still is space for dialogue. North Korea is attempting to prepare a system to secure its regime and check on the U.S. by strengthening relations with China and Russia.

Professor Hiraiwa Shunji from Nanzan University said Japan's policy toward North Korea aims at the normalization of Japan-North Korea relations based on the Pyongyang Declaration. The basic principles of Japan are the comprehensive resolution of nuclear missiles and abductions, international cooperation, and dialogue and pressure. In response to the changes in North Korea's relations with South Korean and the U.S., Japan also is considering normal diplomacy. It is even no longer using the phrase "Maximized pressure" in the U.N. Human Rights Council. According to Shunji, Japan aims to completely denuclearize North Korea. However, it is only considering international cooperation, regardless of North Korea's sincerity and will.

In session 2, Professor Kamo Tomoki from Keio University presented his analysis that the Japan-China relationship is changing from competition to cooperation, and the two countries have stepped to a new stage of further development. Economically, Japan has come to a positive position on China's One Belt, One Road Initiative, for instance, having private economic cooperation with China in the developing world. However, Japan still needs to diversify international risks due to concerns over China's openness, economics, transparency and fiscal soundness. In addition, it has established a military liaison mechanism on the open seas and signed the sea research and rescue agreement that promoted a friendly atmosphere with China, Tomoki said. Nevertheless, the East China Sea is still facing tension.

Professor Kotani Tetsuo from Meikei University compared that while the Obama administration was skeptical and concerned about China's strategic involvement, Trump's public policy has adopted a competitive strategy. It has started strategic competition including trade wars and competition over high-tech and hegemony, he said. He mentioned that U.S.-China competition will last mid to long term, and Japan will stay with the Free and Open Indo-Pacific Initiative that puts more weight on engaging China than checking and competing. There are still concerns about how to face China in 2049 (the centenary of the republic), however, if the U.S. public strategy is Dragon slayer while the Japanese public strategy is Dragon hugger.

Professor Shin Sung-ho from Seoul National University put the current U.S.-China conflict in Asia as the challenge to Korea's strategy on diplomacy and security. Besides directly related and urgent security issues, such as North Korea's nuclear weapons and the THAAD missile defense deployment, South Korea is under pressure from the U.S. and China over various other issues. In this regard, South Korea should not make any choices first, but rather avoid or postpone the situation, Shin said. The country must express its clear stance with rational judgment on what the national interest is. Shin said: "We can build trust in us by presenting principles in accordance with international norms and universal values, together with our national interests. In order to prevent U.S.-China competition from developing into a new cold war between continental and marine forces, we can consider the middle role of Korea-Japan relations".

Published date: 2019. 09. 28

[VIEW]

Belt and Road Initiative: Not a debt trap, but rather a great chance for Sri Lanka

By Jayanath Colombage, Director,
Centre for Indo- Lanka Initiatives
Pathfinder Foundation and Huang Yunsong,
Professor, Sichuan University.

Infrastructure development projects in Sri Lanka, financed with Chinese loans, have become a source of hot debate. It was again cited by United States Vice President Mike Pence as debt-trap diplomacy in his latest accusation against China.

Some arguments, probably based on selective information and wild extrapolations from individual cases, have their own logic as part of a grand strategy against China. However, it doesn't hurt to have a look at the other side of the story, which relies more on empirical factors and factual arguments.

When the separatist conflict for nearly three decades ended in 2009, Sri Lanka felt desperately hungry for economic development. To Sri Lanka's dismay, neither Western democracies nor the immediate neighbor offered to play a major role in its reconstruction or investment in infrastructure, except for several credit lines for housing, hospitals and railways provided by India. Due to the consistent support for Sri Lanka during and after the conflict, China soon became the main development partner and the biggest foreign direct investor.

As the epicenter of the Indian Ocean, Sri Lanka sits right next to one of the busiest shipping lanes in the world. Major maritime powers cannot tolerate China's ambition to take advantage of its strategically important location, not even for economic purposes. This is the main reason for Sri Lanka being singled out to highlight the so-called debt-trap diplomacy of China.

Over the years, Sri Lanka has aspired to be a maritime hub of the Indian Ocean. This concept was developed even before the "Belt and Road Initiative" of China. In 2008, the Sri Lankan government launched the Hambantota port project, based on feasibility studies by several international engineering consultancy firms, such as Ramboll Group A/S of Denmark and SNC Lavalin Inc. of Canada. Before engaging the Chinese company, the project was offered to India. However, India declined the offer due to multiple reasons.

For a three-phase project, there is a considerable gap between completion of the port and starting full commercial operations. The third phase, costing $400-$600 million is due to start at the end of 2018. As such, it was not intended to derive commercial returns soon after the start of operations.

One of the objectives of the port was to provide ancillary services and bunkering operations, which began in 2011. Considering the Indian

Ocean does not have a main bunkering hub, prospects for Hambantota to attract shipping for bunkering should be good, if it could be made competitive and provide a reliable service. However, bunkering operations were stopped in 2015 due to a policy decision, confirming the fact that a stable and favorable political environment is essential for attracting foreign direct investment based on national interests, rather than subjecting such national projects to the vagaries of party politics.

Sri Lanka is in a serious economic predicament due to debt servicing difficulties, which exceed the country's capacity for generating revenue. However, it may be pointed out that Sri Lanka's foreign debt stood at $51.8 billion by December 2017, and China's share was in the region of $8 billion. It is questionable for certain powers to focus attention only on China's loans while neglecting the full picture.

It was alleged that China provided a loan to the Hambantota port project at an excessive interest rate around 6 percent, knowing that there would be insufficient business at the port to repay the debt, with the intention of swapping the debt for equity. On the contrary, according to former President Rajapaksa, $1 billion had been taken at a concessionary rate of 2 percent, and a tranche of $307 million was taken at the London interbank offered rate (LIBOR) plus 0.75 percent, pushing up the interest rate to 6.3 percent. If these figures are accurate, it becomes apparent that the major part of China's loan was taken at a concessionary rate.

China Merchant Port Holdings now owns a 70 percent stake in the Hambantota port for 99 years, with the remaining shares in the hands of Sri Lanka. But it is noteworthy that the lease agreement provides for purchase of shares held by China, if Sri Lanka so decides at a future date.

China's interest in Sri Lanka should be understood in the context of the strong bilateral relations that go far back in history. It is then unsurprising for Sri Lanka to extend support for China's "Belt and Road Initiative".

Rather than debt-trap diplomacy, the true topic here is really about the greatest change at regional and global levels for the past several centuries. When the U.S. works hard to block China's ascendance, Sri Lanka does not want to be dragged into their conflict. Fully aware of the nature of China-India relations, Sri Lanka would never opt to compromise India's security interests by siding with China.

Published date: 2018. 10. 13

[VIEW]

Shangri-La: The silent rebellion of the small powers

By Liselotte Odgaard, Senior Fellow,
Hudson Institute in Washington, D.C.

The 2019 Shangri-La Dialogue was expected to display fireworks between the United States and China. The U.S. announcement of its free and open Indo-Pacific strategy and China's decision to send its defense minister for the first time in eight years set the scene for a wrestling match between the two strategic competitors.

However, the fireworks never came. Indeed, we got a manifestation of the different positions of Washington and Beijing on issues such as Taiwan, the South China Sea and Huawei and 5G. But there was not much interest in putting on display these conflicts by challenging each other in public.

Acting U.S. Secretary of Defense Patrick Shanahan said that what we are witnessing now is not a face-off between the United States and China. Instead, negotiations are taking place on how to prevent military conflict. China's defense minister responded by emphasizing that the militaries of the two powers were acting as stabilizers in the relationship. The fireworks were left to closed-door meetings outside of the public eye.

What is the reason for this self-restraint? Of course, one reason could be that Washington and Beijing are not interested in rocking the boat at a time when they are sounding each other out for a breakthrough in the ongoing trade war. On the other hand, the United States and China seem to be in for the long haul on the trade war, and a defense ministers' meeting is not the main arena for settling this issue.

Another, more subtle reason, which ran as an undercurrent of the speeches of smaller powers, was spelled out by Singapore's defense minister Ng Eng Hen at the very end of the meeting, when half the delegates had already left the dialogue. He said the challenge for the United States and China is to offer acceptance of their dominance beyond military might. If their policies are lopsided against other countries' interests, these countries will seek other partners.

Ng Eng Hen's statement came after a string of defense ministers had gone out of their way to point out that they were not taking sides in the U.S.-Chinese strategic competition. Vietnam's defense minister Ngo Xuan Lich spent a lot of his speaking time emphasizing the excellent platforms for creating a sea of cooperation provided by the Association of Southeast Asian Nations, although ASEAN has little to show for itself when it comes to bringing down tensions in its own home region, as demonstrated by the volatile situation in the South China Sea.

Britain's newly appointed defense minister Penny Mordaunt tried to reassure China by arguing that since the aircraft carrier HMS Queen

Elizabeth's visit to the United States in 2018 was not seen as a threat, nor should its visit in 2022 to the South China Sea be considered as such. Mordaunt's clumsy attempt to convince China that the U.K. will seek to balance relations with the United States and China reflects a general concern among smaller countries to deny being part of U.S. counterbalancing of China. French defense minister Florence Parly mentioned that France had sent its carrier Charles de Gaulle to the Indo-Pacific in 2019 as a force for stability, working with key strategic partners of France such as Singapore, India, Australia, Japan and the U.K., while downplaying the role of the United States and China.

The tendency in Washington and Beijing to try to force allies and partners to choose sides has been growing in the past year. The latest example is the U.S. announcement that Washington cannot share sensitive intelligence with countries that allow Huawei into their telecommunications network. At the same time, China is adopting sanctions against countries such as Australia and New Zealand that have already decided to exclude Huawei. These pressures to choose between Washington and Beijing encourage France, India, South Korea, Singapore, Russia, Australia, Japan and others to look to each other for alternatives to the United States to avoid being caught in the crossfire between the two competitors.

Ng Eng Hen framed this tendency as a warning to the United States and China that they are putting global peace and stability at risk by their unwillingness to compromise on issues of disagreement. However, the tendency for other countries to form alternative partnerships to avoid becoming great power dependents may in fact be what is needed to preserve international order.

For example, the European Union-Japan trade agreement sent a strong signal to the U.S. against unilateralism. The 2019 memorandum of understanding between South Korea and India reflects Seoul's need for partners that will help them pursue diplomatic engagement with North Korea. The rapprochement between Australia and France reflects that Canberra looks for new security partners in the South Pacific.

If looked at separately, these are all small or medium powers that can do little to change the ways of Washington and Beijing. But if added up, together they form a formidable force that can change the trajectory of U.S.-Chinese policies from a preference for bullying their partners and each other to a greater willingness to compromise.

Published date: 2019. 06. 08

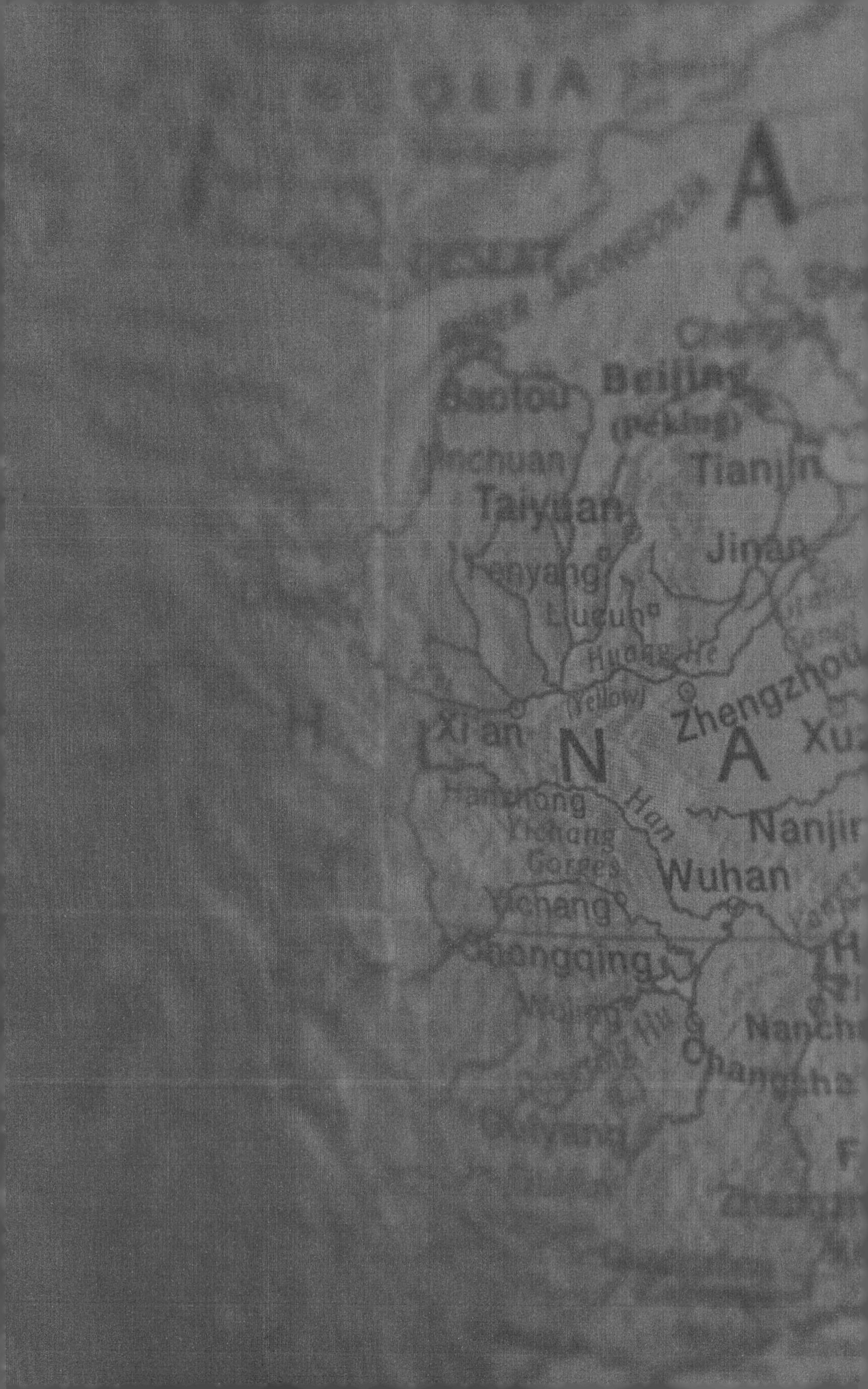
Baotou
Beijing
(Peking)
Tianjin
Taiyuan
Jinan
(Yellow)
Zhengzhou
Xi'an
Han
Wuhan
Gorges

2

Korea's Foreign Relations

China Watcher

2 Korea's Foreign Relations

2. 1. South Korea and China

[VIEW]

China still matters

By Jaeho Hwang, Professor, Hankuk University of Foreign Studies, Seoul.

On May 4, a week after the Inter-Korean Summit, President Moon Jae-in and President Xi Jinping finally held their first phone conversation. No one knows whether Moon had tried to phone earlier, but the result was quite pleasing because both agreed on close cooperation during the process of "Declaration of the end of war" and "Peace Treaty".

Although the recent online conversation eased the controversy regarding the "China Passing (isolation)", we again witnessed how challenging and susceptible the road to peace can be; what we went through with China this time has become an effective vaccination for the further big picture, the "Peace Regime".

Nevertheless, when we analyze realistically what happened two weeks ago, China had focused more on its "Mongni (avarice)" rather than "Passing". "Passing" basically refers to "Isolation". However, in terms of dynamics, structures, and circumstances, the actual possibility of excluding China is very low.

China has will and capability to utilize various measures to manipulate the contents of a "Peace Regime" and to slow it down as well. If China is dissatisfied with how the situation is shaping, it can distort and complicate things whenever it wishes.

China is not making a song and dance about it, but considers it has made considerable efforts to bring about the current situation on the Korean Peninsula. Because China was the key to sanctions on North Korea, which is also a burden to China, what the U.S. is getting in return is thought to be unfair.

The "Panmunjom Declaration", in which the U.S. and the two Koreas seem to have had the determinant roles, with China as a bit player, was an unpleasant event for Beijing. So the following advice might be useful in regard to China.

First, we should emphasize that the three-party talks (the U.S., South and North Korea) is a simple interim-station, while the four-party talks (the U.S., China, South and North Korea) are the final destination. It should be emphasized that the three-party talks will actually speed up the "Peace Regime". With denuclearization on the table, this would leave China in a difficult position if it objects. China cannot deny that progress should move rapidly to cope with Trump's unpredictability. Otherwise China will be stigmatized as behaving selfishly.

Second, explain that South Korea's actual role in the three-party talks is more of a buffer to assist in the U.S.-North Korean Summit. If the Panmunjom Declaration was the declaration of the end of war between two

Koreas, the declaration in the three-party talks is de facto a declaration of the end of war between the U.S. and North Korea. South Korea is just coordinating things to ensure a successful outcome.

Third, there must be ongoing efforts to placate China's suspicions. South Korea must build trust by including China in the process and genuinely making sure Beijing is fully informed about the three-party talks. Korea must suggest and support new six-party talks including China, the U.S. and both Koreas, so everyone works together toward the "Peace Regime".

I believe Japan and Russia must also be invited to the table. For example, the U.S. and both Koreas could be directly involved as the signing countries in the Declaration Ceremony, while the ministers or envoys from China, Japan, and Russia attend as observers? Or perhaps the U.S., China, and both Koreas could sign while Japan and Russia attend as observers?

Because the neighboring powers have their own issues, we cannot solely concentrate on North Korean denuclearization. In the other words, if South Korea offers sufficient methods and agendas for building the "Peace Regime", it would naturally lead and speed the process. But if only the U.S. and the two Koreas declared the end of war, extra effort and time will be needed to prepare the Peace Treaty. In short, gathering all the interested states simultaneously in one place is one solution to make things as easy as possible.

It would reflect credit upon the interest states that essentially need to

participate. Furthermore, it would provide a sense of belonging and responsibility. Considering and doing our duty by inviting all the interested parties beforehand will be a positive step for now and the future.
Let us finally have a peace treaty that finally brings an end to this long, long war.

One factor that largely contributed to German unification was a sustainable communication and trust-building program with neighboring countries. Only proper firepower and time can cook a nice meal, otherwise it will be overcooked or undercooked. Once the meal is perfectly cooked, a permanent and concrete "Peace Regime" can be established.

Published date: 2018. 05. 15

[VIEW]

Inter-Korean summit and China's role

By Jaeho Hwang, Professor, Hankuk University of Foreign Studies, Seoul.

Tomorrow (Apr. 27), President Moon Jae-in and north Korean leader Kim Jong-un are holding a sensational summit at Panmunjeom, the village which represents the division of the two Koreas. Following the summits of Kim Jong-il with Kim Dae-Jung, and Kim Jong-il with Roh Moo-Hyun, this is the third summit between leaders from the South and North.

This time it has several significant points; first, from a short term perspective, it could bring about sustainable and regularized Inter-Korean talks as well as a successful U.S.-North Korea Summit; second, it could be the beginning of peace building on the Korean Peninsula over the long term. The ultimate purpose of the April 27 summit is way more meaningful than a simple meeting between the two Koreas' leaders; it is a symbolic but practical process for denuclearization, a mutual agreement on principles regarding the peace regime, a military detente and trust-building measures, and exchanges and cooperation on a civic level can be anticipated. The core of the summit is peace and security.

First, a remark about denuclearization directly from Kim Jong-un will clear up not only North Korea's will and promise on denuclearization, but also the meaning of the gradual and conditional denuclearization North Korea has mentioned. Second, the further disposal of ICBMs, which is of critical interest to the U.S., can be confirmed. Though a practical dismantlement, verification and inspection of North Korea's denuclearization must be the best case, at least we will get to know North Korea's position on "CVID". Third, it will be an opportunity to tap the necessity for a newly upgraded Six-party Talks framework, and the potential possibility for North Korea's reinstatement in them. Fourth, the current Korean peninsula status and related multilateral security will be comprehensively discussed regarding the peace regime. Fifth, an approach which accompanies the denuclearization in a virtuous cycle might be recommended. Summing up, in order to settle a peace regime on detente, a symbolic and substantial outcome needs to be derived.

Besides the security issue, exchanges and cooperation in sport, culture and art will be revitalized. In addition, along with efforts on specifying and expanding humanitarian aid, considerable positive impacts will spill over to unexpected sectors. However, since South Korea's independent economic cooperation with North Korea is not feasible under current international sanctions on the North, the approach will be cautiously held to a limited, selective, and gradual way.

Nevertheless, the pace and the spectrum of the field are expected to increase depending on the results of the U.S.-North Korea Summit. As soon as the inter-Korean meeting ends, the government must be ready to get back to reality, preparing for later circumstances.

Coordinating the potential obstacles of U.S.-North Korea Summit is a priority. To begin with, prior consultations regarding denuclearization and a peace regime should be delivered to the U.S. in order to successfully complete the talks. Furthermore, a plan needs to be established to implement any inter-Korean agreement while maintaining and institutionalizing the inter-Korean communication channel at the same time.

Above all, the agenda and systems for various measures should be arranged: U.S.-South-North Korea, China-South-North Korea, U.S.-China-South-North Korea talks or others. In this sense, another Inter-Korean Summit after the U.S-North Korea Summit is a crucial necessity. So far, China and both Koreas have been the main actors in Korean peninsula issues; however, this was converted into the U.S. and two Koreas leading during the PyeongChang Olympics.

An uncomfortable situation for China referred to as "China Passing" has taken place. In spite of such dynamics, China's role as ever remains critical in that North Korea will not change without its participation. In other words, China is still the key-player here as we witnessed through the China-North Korea Summit.

The international condition requires China's more clear and expanded role. For instance, it should adhere to its present standpoint toward North Korea until the U.S.-North Korea Summit, in order to prove it has not released any of the sanctions on the North. Since the "Freeze for Freeze" and the "Dual-Track Approach" is actually going on, implicit cooperation with South Korea is essential to sustain these routes. Before actual multilateral talks, China must work on determining the form of a peace regime agreement: either U.S.-South-North Korea combination which allows China's guarantee or a U.S.-China-South-North Korea simultaneously.

Today's Northeast Asia is very complicated, adding North Korea issues to the U.S.'s diplomacy, security and trade policies toward China and South Korea. Considering Trump's personal political crisis and the off-year election in November, both the U.S.-China and U.S.-South Korea relations are unpredictable. China should promote foreign policies which receive positive perceptions in South Korea. In South Korea, on the other hand, China is often recognized as an irresponsible defect in sanctions on North Korea or is supportive to North Korea. Therefore, until a tangible outcome in North Korea is proven, it seems necessary to make China a close and reliable friend of South Korea, China as a responsible power.

Published date: 2018. 04. 26

[VIEW]

On the second Trump-Kim summit: China hopes for solid progress

By Yang Xiangfeng, Assistant Professor,
Yonsei University.

How time flies. And how different a year can be. This time last year the world was still very much unsure what would unfold amid Kim Jong-un's Olympic charm offensive after the "Fire and fury" of 2017. But now we are on the cusp of witnessing a second summit between Kim and U.S. President Donald Trump.

A year ago, Chinese officials, still trying to charm and being charmed by Trump, did not see the trade war coming; and now they are working hard to see the end of it. Apropos Korean affairs in particular, several broad observations jump out.

First, a great deal of what was said or implied by Beijing about its relations with North Korea seems to have lost its relevance. After years of characterizing Sino-DPRK relations as "Normal state-to-state" relations, since 2018 Beijing has dropped the "Normal" reference, as Kim's denuclearization pledge removed the biggest obstacle between them. In their meetings, whereas Kim Jong-un appeared to dutifully ingratiate himself with his host, Xi Jinping went to great lengths to emphasize the enduring Chinese devotion to the North Korean party, people and state.

Second, for all the suggestions that North Korea was a sovereign nation making its own decisions, especially when Pyongyang defied its wishes, Beijing can no longer convincingly claim that it has no influence on Pyongyang's behaviour. Such sentiment cannot be made more emphatically than by Robert Kelly, an American scholar based in South Korea, who, in the wake of news breaking on Kim's first visit to Beijing in late March, argued that "Next time, the Chinese ministry of foreign affairs says the real issue is between the U.S. and North Korea, and that China is just a mediator or just wants stability, we will know they are lying". In fact, in the past couple of years, Chinese influence was placed on full display — positive in the form, for example, of the Air China plane that flew Kim to his history-making rendezvous with Trump, and negative in the sense that its cooperation was indispensable in Trump's maximum-pressure campaign against North Korea.

Third, the intertwining of China's relations with North Korea and the United States is now a matter of indisputable fact. In a dramatic yet also perfectly understandable way, the Xi-Kim meetings have been serving as a good indicator — or even predictor, as in the case of their January 2019 meeting — of the Kim-Trump summits. The same days (in January 2019) when Kim paid his fourth visit to China in 10 months, the U.S. delegation was also in Beijing to negotiate a deal to end the trade spat. And now it looks like Trump will meet Xi somewhere right after seeing Kim in Vietnam.

By no means was Trump the only one — as he often did after Singapore — to raise suspicion and lodge complaints that Beijing intended to sabotage the Pyongyang-Washington thaw to get Washington to compromise on trade. Whereas the Foreign Ministry spokesperson publicly mocked that claim, my sense is that Chinese leaders are too eager to manage the fallout of the trade war — whose impact has been more damaging to the Chinese economy than perhaps expected — to mix the two issues in their dealings with the Trump administration, so much so that the case of Huawei's top executive's arrest in Vancouver at the behest of Washington has seen Chinese authorities mostly train their ire on Canada.

But Chinese activism on the peninsula is not to be denied. Besides arriving on his birthday, Kim's January sojourn to Beijing was noted by some official sources for several "Details" of great distinction that included his warm reception by the host, the make-up of his entourage, his itinerary and the subjects of discussion between the two sides.

Beneath all those excessive expressions of mutual love and respect, however, even the most ardently pro-DPRK scholar was clear-eyed about the geopolitical underpinning of the fast warming of the relationship from deep freeze just two years ago. Short on specifics, other analysts have not shied away either from linking Kim's audience with Xi and his then unannounced second meeting with Trump. The key word they preferred is "Coordination" of positions of all sides without giving the impression that the Xi-Kim meeting was aimed at targeting the U.S. A further common thread of interests (or hope) is that Kim's tour of a factory and the inclusion of some key economic officials in the trip are clear signs North Korea is serious about prioritizing economic development.

Moving forward, the Chinese approach is quite clear. On one hand, having repaired its relations with Pyongyang on Kim's promise to denuclearize, China has no appetite to continue the pressure campaign against its nominal ally. Instead, it is back to the inducement track adopted in the last years of Kim Jong-il. On the other hand, the Chinese side hopes to see more progress at the Kim-Trump meeting in Vietnam.

Given that they have reached some sort of understanding with North Korea, Beijing clearly wants to see Washington compromise on Pyongyang's terms with respect to sanction relief and confidence-building measures. A Global Times editorial, for example, urged Washington to "Shoulder the responsibilities it deserves, and absorb the cost that it should undertake". These expectations and sentiments, however, are not new. What remains to be seen is what happens in Vietnam and what actions Beijing might take to ease the pain caused to North Korea by the sanctions mandated by the Security Council.

Published date: 2019. 02. 23

2. 2. South Korea and the US

[VIEW]

Trump is a nobleman, at least on the Korean Peninsula

By Jaeho Hwang, Professor,
Hankuk University of Foreign Studies, Seoul.

The world's attention is on Singapore, where the U.S.-DPRK summit will be held on June 12. It is also where the world's largest security dialogue, the Shangri-la Dialogue, was held. The topic of this year's security dialogue was, as expected, the Korean peninsula along with Indo-Pacific strategy, which was addressed by the keynote speaker, Indian Prime Minister Narendra Modi. Until the present day, the situation on the Korean peninsula was always hard to be defined because it kept changing. The international community was thrown off guard due to the political imaginations of the leaders of North Korea, South Korea, and the U.S.

Nevertheless, the huge change on the Korean peninsula is now a reality. The strong uncertainty and instability that comes to mind when we hear the name "Trump" is likely to disappear, especially among experts and the media. Uncertainty still exists at a micro level including his behavior patterns, but now it is no longer at the macro level where he aims to make compromises through deals.

Based on this certainty, the U.S.-DPRK summit is likely to be somewhat successful. We will be able to find the definition of full denuclearization and find ways for a good negotiation. It will be a victory for Donald Trump while still being able to provide substantial consideration to Kim Jung-un. Trump must achieve enough to win in the U.S. mid-term election and Kim Jung-un will take action in his own way. In other words, on the outside, it will take the form of a package settlement with the inside being a phased and simultaneous settlement.

As Trump mentioned, there may be more than one U.S.-DPRK summit. Summits of various combinations are possible. Of course, Trump must always be in the center. It is hard to rule out completely the possibility of a tripartite summit between North Korea, South Korea and the U.S. happening on the June 13 if the U.S.-DPRK summit on June 12h goes well. If Trump stands in the middle with North Korea and South Korea at his side declaring the end of war, it will be a historical scene. Even if this picture is not made this time, it will be made soon in one format or another.

South Korean President Moon Jae-in has contributed greatly to changing the course of history. In May, when he came to power, there were some worries due to the existence of strong leaders of neighboring countries, especially because Moon had a weak image in terms of leadership. However, his "Iron hand in a velvet glove" foreign diplomacy made surrounding nations acknowledge him as a safe driver.

If the end of the war declaration is made at the U.S.-DPRK summit in Singapore or sometime later, then the discussion for the next day will focus on the peace treaty. From that time onwards, China will be in full swing. Over the past year, China was the main player, even though invisible. It will be seen more often on the stage now. In the Panmunjom Declaration, there was an expression that the end of war declaration and the peace treaty will only be made between three parties, the U.S., South Korea, and North Korea, or four parties including China. This brought about the "China passing" controversy both domestically and internationally, but this is actually an expression that overlooked China's role. China's decision to join economic sanctions against North Korea brought North Korea to the negotiation table. China has only been stepping aside to put the spotlight on Trump. China will now return.

It is regrettable that Japan is showing an ambiguous stance, but nothing more or less than that. The issue of kidnapping or medium-range missiles will have to be solved at the North-Japan summit by preparing a large amount of reparations for its former colony. In the midst of South Korea, North Korea, the U.S. and China are avoiding mentioning human rights issues and U.S. forces in Korea, and Japan will not be able to make excessive demands of the U.S. Russia is also making preparations as can be seen from its foreign minister's visit North Korea and meeting with Kim Jong-un. In the end, the Korean peninsula will return to the framework of the new six-party talks. It will be upgraded to ministerial level rather than the previous, vice-ministerial level, and depending on the agenda, combinations of bilateral, tripartite, or four-party talks will be made within this frame.

Trump is not the leader we have seen so far. He is not an orthodox boxer but an anomalistic one. Perhaps history is made by thoughts and actions of atypical people like him. He is already an historical tycoon; he is not an eccentric but a nobleman, at least in the Korean Peninsula. I earnestly hope to hear good news from Singapore soon.

Published date: 2018. 06. 10

[VIEW]

U.S.-China trade dispute, evaluation and Korea's choice

By Lim Ho-yeol, Professor, Kyonggi University.

After the U.S. raised the tariff rate on Chinese products worth $200 billion to 25 percent, China responded with a counter-punch, imposing retaliatory tariffs up to 25 percent on $60 billion of U.S. products.

As the U.S. surpassed the tipping point, China declared it would fight against the U.S., saying on state-run media CCTV: "To the Chinese people who have endured 5,000 years of heavy wind and rain, there is no hardship they cannot face".

Due to the trade war between the two superpowers, world trade is sharply declining and the economy is showing signs of a steep downturn. Some even predict that the nightmare of the 1930s, which led to the Great Depression, may return.

This year marks the 40th anniversary of diplomatic relations between the U.S. and China. When China joined the World Trade Organization (WTO) in 2001, it entered the global supply chain cautiously, like a Chinese woman with bound feet. Since then, China has faithfully adapted to U.S.

platforms such as Windows and Android, emerging as a production powerhouse that covers a quarter of the world's manufacturing output — all in less than two decades.

These days, China has grown into a manufacturing global value chain (GVC) hub, larger than the U.S. and Germany. This is clearly different from other emerging economies' participation in the Western-led GVC. For the U.S., which prides itself as a leading player in the global economy, it would not want to tolerate and rely on the presence of GVCs led by China. However, it is undeniable that the U.S. is already relying on the China-led GVC: it is China's biggest importer.

Looking back, China completed its catch-up strategy in pursuit of industrialization by imitating the technology of advanced countries in the early stage of opening up, and has now begun implementing the so-called "Leapfrogging strategy", a dynamic comparative advantage strategy that overtook advanced countries.

A case in point is the "Made in China 2025" strategy for industrial advancement, which sparked trade disputes in the high-tech industry, the basis of U.S. national power. Competition for future technology over the economic hegemony has been created.

From such a perspective, even if the current U.S.-China trade dispute is settled, it is obvious that disputes will recur. The latest U.S.-China trade war may be nothing more than a local battle in the early stages of a decades-long economic war.

China is no longer locked into a U.S.-designed platform and is creating its own China standard. For example, Chinese-type platforms and technical standards are emerging, such as the open-source mobile ecosystem Alipay, DJI's technical standards that control 70 percent of the world's civilian drone market, Huawei's 5G, and the Compass satellite navigation system that responds to America's GPS.

The results are also formidable. QR code payments have quickly lifted China from a financially underdeveloped country to an advanced fintech country, and Huawei's telecommunications equipment dominates the global market.

The miniaturization of drones is also evolving into a technology that tracks and captures moving objects while converging with unmanned technologies. China, which has the world's largest delivery market, is upgrading drones to remote robots in agriculture and disaster areas. It is creating new technology standards and ecosystems as its seamless communications technology, recognition and control sensors and the cloud system of Alibaba, the world's fifth-largest, converge.

The economic potential of China is also growing. China is stepping up efforts to localize technologies to break through the U.S.-China trade dispute, indicating the possibility of a new phase in development. According to patent application records (KISTA, 2005-17), China ranks first in the world in four of the five key areas of the Fourth Industrial Revolution, i.e. internet of things (IOT), big data, 3D printing and intelligent robots, excluding AI.

China had called for the re-establishment of financial order in the Bretton Woods system designed by Anglo-Saxon countries based on the rapid growth of manufacturing industry. China launched a new financial order called the Asian Infrastructure Investment Bank (AIIB) in 2016 after the IMF and World Bank failed to respond to changes. The Asian Development Bank (ADB), founded in 1966, has only 68 member countries, but the AIIB has gained 97 members in its first three years. Also, sources say the investment volume reached $10 billion by end of April 2019.

What is the impact of the U.S.-China conflict on Korean national interests? First of all, if the U.S. presses China further, China's exports to the U.S. will shrink and Korea's exports — which account for 78 percent of its exports of intermediate goods to China — will face a severe negative impact. Of course, some items, such as mobile phones, TVs and electronics, which are highly competitive with China, may benefit in exports to the U.S.

Industrial competition between Korea and China is also likely to intensify. This is because the world factory will move from China to Vietnam or India faster. China will try to reorganize its industries with a high value-added focus like Korea's. Korea needs to speed up the development of new technologies before China catches up.

Our choice is also becoming more difficult even in the international trade order. Some argue that Korea should walk on an agile rope, choosing sides case-by-case between the U.S. and China. In my opinion, Korea should join the CATPP trade agreement before it's too late, as costs of joining will rise significantly when the U.S. returns to negotiations. In the future, the world will see a recruiting competition between the two superpowers, and nations will split and join according to national interests. Korea should tread with caution so as not to be drawn into this competition and be practical in its decisions.

Published date: 2019. 05. 18

[VIEW]

Winners and losers after Trump's DMZ visit

By Yoon Suk-joon, Senior Fellow,
Korea Institute for Military Affairs.

On June 30, U.S. President Donald Trump and North Korean leader Kim Jong-un crossed a line dividing the South and North Korean parts of Panmunjeom in the Demilitarized Zone (DMZ). Trump thus became the first sitting U.S. president to step onto North Korean soil.

Also present was South Korean President Moon Jae-In, who is keen to help mediate between the U.S. and North Korea in hopes of reviving stalled denuclearization talks after the debacle of the abandoned February Hanoi summit.

This unprecedented three-way summit, apparently arranged at very short notice, appears to have been little more than a made-for-TV spectacular designed for Trump and Kim's domestic audiences, in the military conflict zone of the Korean Peninsula.

Trump's publicity machine constantly emphasizes the feel-good, one-to-one personal relationship between Trump and Kim, but is there any actual progress on denuclearization? Supposedly, this meeting will lead to a resumption of working-level talks, but there are clear indications that the U.S. side is no longer committed to "Complete, verifiable, irreversible denuclearization".

So what does Chairman Kim get from the meeting? It seems he is closer to persuading Trump to accept the North Korean agenda. no pressure for regime change or reform, and a freeze on North Korea's missile and nuclear program instead of a ban. This would essentially enshrine the status quo on the Korean Peninsula and would tacitly recognize North Korea as a nuclear power. Probably it means that the dismantling of the Yongbyon nuclear facility will be traded for the partial lifting of United Nations Security Council (UNSC) sanctions against North Korea. Clearly Kim is a big winner from the meeting.

And what about President Moon? Despite his broad smiles during the photo session, he seems ready to make significant concessions to the U.S. and North Korea. Instead of maintaining a balanced stance between the two regional great powers, Moon may intend to toe the U.S. line more assiduously. For example, by joining in with sanctions against Huawei, by participating in U.S.-led freedom of navigation operations in the South China Sea, by buying more U.S.-made weapons and systems to ensure interoperability for a combined military posture toward North Korea, and by increased burden-sharing to support the U.S. military presence. Any such concessions would reveal Moon as the greatest loser from the meeting.

Lastly there is Trump to consider. He successfully distracted attention from his utter failure to achieve even the tiniest step toward North Korean denuclearization by pretending that his personal relationship with Kim is some kind of historic accomplishment. Kim, of course, is happy to indulge this pathetic charade, since he is playing the same game. Moreover, by focusing the attention of U.S. TV screens on foreign policy, Trump also displaced coverage of his democratic opponents' presidential primary campaigns and of the continuing investigations into his own conduct. All-in-all this meeting was a big win for Trump.

So, putting this eye-catching TV show to one side, what is actually happening now on the Korean Peninsula? There are several important questions outstanding.

First, is there any prospect that we may finally escape from the military standoff that has blighted the peninsula for almost seven decades? The U.S. and the Koreas are still involved in continuing military frictions, which might easily escalate into the nightmare scenario of a major confrontation. And as yet there is no hint of conventional arms control or reduction, never mind the North Korean nuclear capabilities. All that has happened is the scaling-down of bilateral joint military drills between the ROK armed forces and U.S. Forces Korea (USFK), and a weakening of their combined defense posture through the decision to transfer of wartime operational control authority from USFK to the South Korean military no later than 2021.

Since the signing of an agreement between the two Korean militaries in September 2018, there has also been some work to recover the remains of U.S. personnel missing in action, but none of this has changed the facts on the ground: peace has not broken out on the Korean Peninsula, where the Cold War continues.

Second, is it time to sign a peace treaty to finally end the Korean War after an uneasy truce that has lasted many decades? The three leaders' meeting at Panmunjeom should remind us that the Korean Peninsula is divided into two countries with competing ideologies and remains technically at war. Thus, Trump was escorted by U.S. soldiers of the United Nations Command, their commander now dual-hatted and in charge of both ROK-U.S. Combined Forces Command and USFK.

Anyone who believes that war is now unlikely or impossible is ignoring North Korean and Chinese policy that has always insisted on a complete withdrawal of all foreign troops from the Korean Peninsula. Does this suggest that China will leave Koreans to determine their own affairs? Surely President Moon is not so naive, and though his earnest pursuit of a genuine Korean peace process may be laudable, it is not yet practicable, because none of the other parties are acting in good faith.

Third, is there now no possibility that North Korean nuclear warheads and missile delivery systems can be removed? Most observers believe the best that can be achieved is a freeze in the continuing development of North Korean nuclear capabilities and that full denuclearization is an unrealistic fantasy, since the North Korean regime relies on its nuclear deterrent for its very survival.

So, North Korea will retain the ability to threaten U.S. cities with nuclear weapons for the indefinite future, yet Trump's failure goes beyond this disturbing reality, since even if he was discussing a nuclear freeze in his meeting with Kim, North Korea is yet to provide a comprehensive listing of all North Korean nuclear assets and facilities, and without this any freeze would be a joke. Kim was happy to show up in Panmunjeom without working-level negotiations on denuclearization, because he does not intend to denuclearize, ever. It is improbable that North Korea would adhere even to an agreed nuclear freeze, though its current stock of perhaps 20-60 nuclear bombs is already sufficient to achieve recognition as a nuclear power, uncomfortable though that is for South Korea, and even for China. The situations of India, Pakistan and Israel are all different, but in every case the possession of an effective nuclear deterrent has resulted in permanent geopolitical shifts.

Fourth, is there any substance whatever behind the summit of the three leaders? Could personal diplomacy between Trump and Kim perhaps moderate Trump's capriciousness, making erratic military action by Trump less likely? But domestic politics is surely the driving force behind the meeting. Trump needs a foreign policy success (even a faked one will do for his base) to help his reelection campaign. Kim gets to pose as an equal with the U.S. President, to his newly reshuffled team and to the North Korean people. And Moon gets the benefit of diverting South Koreans' attention from historical and economic frictions with Japan and China; by presenting himself as a peacemaker he hopes to win a majority in the coming National Assembly elections. For the present, there is no indication that anyone is serious about the kind of diplomacy that is needed to find the long-term flexible solutions that regional security requires and on which the peace and prosperity of the Korean Peninsula depends.

In summary: The Panmunjeom meeting of June 30 between President Trump and Chairman Kim, with President Moon as facilitator, was a triumph of presentation over substance and delivered very much less than it promised. The military standoff on the Korean Peninsula continues unabated, no one is serious about a genuine peace treaty, no progress whatever was made toward North Korean denuclearization and all of the leaders demonstrated their hypocrisy, though Moon showed more sincerity than Trump or Kim. The meeting was a shallow exercise in personal promotion by the respective leaders for their domestic ends. It was a TV entertainment spectacular and feel-good moment that made no useful contribution to the urgent and dire problems of the Korean Peninsula, whose people are the starkest losers from this fiasco.

Published date: 2019. 07. 13

2. 3. South Korea and Japan

[INTERVIEW]

Korea-Japan relations: Against all odds, there is still hope

With Nagamine Yasumasa, Japanese Ambassador to Korea.

By Jaeho Hwang

Korea-Japan relations are without a doubt one of the most important bilateral relationships for the two countries. The rosiest period for both might have been October 1998 when former Korean President Kim Dae Jung and then Japanese Prime Minister Keizo Obuchi issued in Tokyo a "Japan-Republic of Korea (ROK) Joint Declaration: A New Japan-ROK Partnership toward the Twenty-first Century" comprised of 11 articles.

Prime Minister Obuchi expressed "His deep remorse and heartfelt apology" for the tremendous damage and suffering to the people of Korea during the colonial period (1910-1945). President Kim, in turn, accepted with sincerity this statement of Obuchi's recognition of history and expressed his appreciation for it. He also expressed his view that the present calls for both countries to overcome their unfortunate history and to build a future-oriented relationship based on reconciliation and friendly cooperation.

Today, 20 years after the joint declaration, ties between the two countries, including people-to-people exchanges and economic cooperation, have strengthened dramatically. We have more than 10 million people coming and going between Japan and Korea. However, it is truly unfortunate that bilateral relations are challenged by various issues that have happened in Korea, such as judgments by the Korean Supreme Court, "Comfort women" or labour statues, territorial disputes and so on. Under such circumstances, Professor Jaeho Hwang of Hankuk University of Foreign Studies sat down at the Japanese Embassy in Seoul with H.E. Nagamine Yasumasa, the Japanese Ambassador to Korea, to ask about the future for the two countries.

Q. As Emperor Naruhito ascended the throne, the new Reiwa era has begun. What is Japan like after the change?

A. The last 30 years of Heisei was the era in which peace was maintained in and out of Japan, while Japan also experienced major economic changes and natural disasters. The new emperor ascended the throne on May 1 and the new era of Reiwa has started. Reiwa is a combination of Rei, meaning beautiful, and Wa, meaning harmony, and it represents the sentiment that a culture comes into being and flourishes when people bring their hearts and minds in a beautiful manner. The Japanese people congratulate the coming of a new era and hope that in the rapidly changing international situation the era of Reiwa will be peaceful, hopeful and harmonious.

Q. What would be the foremost issue for the reconciliation of Korea-Japan relations?

A. The issue surrounding the former laborers from the Korean Peninsula is very serious. The judgments by the Supreme Court of Korea last year ordered Japanese companies to pay compensation to those former workers from the Korean Peninsula, which is against the 1965 Japan-Korea Agreement that stipulates that the problem concerning claims is settled completely and finally. The judgments clearly violate international law. However, the plaintiffs asked that the assets of Japanese companies be seized and also announced that they would seek the sale of those assets. Under such circumstances, the Japanese government has notified of a decision about arbitration? to the Korean government.

Q. The plaintiffs who won the compensation case against the Japanese companies applied for the sale of the seized assets. How would the Japanese government react if the assets were to be sold?

A. I do not think it is necessary to discuss a matter that has not yet happened and I would like to avoid mentioning what might happen and when. However, if it were to come to that, then Japan would not accept the unjust selling of the Japanese companies' assets and it would affect bilateral economic relations as well as the Korean economy. Even though the Japanese government seeks arbitration, there will be room for Korea to improvise a more concrete resolution to the issue.

Q. Prime Minister Abe has been a strong advocate for North Korean denuclearization. But he has recently offered an unconditional summit meeting with the North Korean leader Kim Jong-un. Has there been a change in pressure on North Korea using sanctions?

A. PM Abe has always supported his willingness to meet Chairman Kim and break the mistrust between North Korea and Japan in order to solve the abduction issue. The comment on the unconditional summit meeting only reflects his willingness even clearer. Japan still aims to resolve the

various issues, including that of abductees, nuclear arms and missiles, based on the Japan-North Korean Declaration in Pyongyang, to settle the unfortunate past and normalize the bilateral relationship.

Q. I personally think that the leaders of both Korea and Japan should meet in person to resolve these issues. Could there be a Korea-Japan summit meeting on the occasion of the G20 in Osaka this June?

A. Nothing is set at this moment and I hope to avoid any presupposition.

Q. Even though the bilateral diplomatic relationship is not at its best, tourism between the two countries is the biggest yet. What are your thoughts on this?

A. Last year, Korean visitors to Japan reached 7.54 million while the total number of visitors between Korea and Japan recorded its highest of over 10 million. The booming tourism is positive in that it promotes mutual understanding at the citizen level. Recently, there has been an increase in number of Japanese restaurants in Seoul and Japanese products, such as Japanese drinks and desserts, are highly popular among Korean youth. Likewise, K-pop is extremely popular among young Japanese people. Our embassy plans to support people-to-people exchanges in various areas with diverse age groups and classes even more in the future.

Q. The Japanese economy is booming to the degree of the pre-war period. There are some Korean young people wishing to seek employment in Japan due to high unemployment at home.

A. Japan and Korea are each other's third-biggest trade partner and one of the biggest investors for one another. The semiconductor industry, which is the core industry for the Korean economy, is the area where many bilateral exchanges are taking place and supporting the Korean semiconductor industry as a whole, with many Japanese companies supplying equipment and materials for semiconductor production. On the other hand, I do hope that Korean consumers gain a correct understanding of safety of Japanese products and that the import regulation is abolished so Korean citizens can enjoy safe and delicious Japanese produce.

Q. What would you say is the happiest occasion as Japanese ambassador to Korea in the past three years?

A. The happiest occasion is when I visit charming cities of Korea outside Seoul and have a chance to have a conversation with many Koreans. I feel so touched whenever I discover the cultural similarities and differences between Japan and Korea

Q. Is there anything you want to add as to future-oriented Korea-Japan relations?

A. Japan and Korea are friends that help one another in need and they should be that. The Korean government and the citizens of Korea offered their help to Japan faced with catastrophe and I am still highly appreciative of that fact. Japan and Korea are both facing challenges of a low birth rate, aging population and disaster prevention, among others, and I hope we can cooperate more in these regards.

Published date: 2019. 06. 22

[INTERVIEW]

'Korea, Japan indispensable to each other'

With Narushige Michishit, Professor, National Graduate Institute for Policy Studies.

By Jaeho Hwang

As a representative specialist in Japanese security and foreign policy as well as security issues on the Korean Peninsula, Narushige Michishita is vice president and professor at the National Graduate Institute for Policy Studies (GRIPS) in Tokyo.

He is a member of the National Security Secretariat Advisory Board of the Government of Japan and a global fellow at the Woodrow Wilson International Center for Scholars in Washington DC. He has served as senior research fellow at Japan's National Institute for Defense Studies (NIDS), Ministry of Defense, and as assistant counselor at the Cabinet Secretariat for Security and Crisis Management of the Government of Japan. He acquired his Ph.D. from the School of Advanced International Studies (SAIS), Johns Hopkins University. In August 13, he sat with me to discuss the current status and way forward for regional security.

Q. People in South Korea think that the US-Japan relationship is in good shape. Are they right?

A. US-Japan relations are good but we face two challenges. First, Japanese security specialists think that the ability of the United States to maintain peace and stability in the Indo-Pacific region will decline over time due largely to the rise of China. According to the Stockholm International Peace Research Institute, China's defense expenditure has grown by 83 percent in the past decade while that of the United States has declined by 17 percent. The trend is clear: the United States will not be the predominant power in this region forever.

Second, President Trump is highly unpredictable. In May, Prime Minister Abe invited Mr. Trump as a state guest and gave him a big treat. The two leaders were smiling and shaking hands. Then in June, it was reported that Mr. Trump had discussed possible withdrawal from the U.S.-Japan alliance with his confidants. He also burst out in a TV interview and said, "If Japan is attacked, we will fight World War III. But if we're attacked, Japan doesn't have to help us. They can watch it on a Sony television". Mr. Abe is doing his best to maintain an amicable relationship with Mr. Trump, but there is a limit to what he can do.

Q. If the United States is not reliable, what will Japan do to deal with China?

A. Japan's approach to China is simple: cooperate and compete. Japan has already changed its approach to China's Belt and Road Initiative (BRI). Although skeptical at first, Japan reversed course and started to cooperate with China on BRI. Last year, President Xi Jinxing and Mr. Abe agreed to embark on "Third country cooperation", a coded term for cooperation on BRI projects devised to save Japan's face.

While they cooperate, they also compete. Japan has started to make an asymmetric region-wide response, defying China's hegemonic attempts not only in the East China Sea but also in the South China Sea and the Indian Ocean. For example, Japanese naval vessels have visited ports in Malaysia, Brunei, and Sri Lanka in recent years. These are the ports where China's influence is becoming more visible.

Last year, a Japanese helicopter carrier, two destroyers, and a submarine conducted an anti-submarine warfare exercise in the South China Sea, inside China's controversial "Nine-dash line". The message was clear: the South China Sea is open and free, and no country can monopolize it.

Q. North Korea has started launching missiles again. What kind of threat does North Korea pose to Japan and how is Japan responding?
A. When it comes to North Korea's threat, South Korea, Japan and the United States are in the same boat. If something bad happens on the Korean Peninsula, the United States will intervene on the South Korean side, and Japan will provide operating bases for the U.S. forces and the Japanese armed forces will likely support U.S. combat operations.

North Korea has developed nuclear weapons and medium- to long-range missiles partly to drive a wedge between South Korea on the one hand and the United States and Japan on the other hand. Japan has spent about $18 billion on ballistic missile defense systems to fend off such an attempt.

On the positive side, North Korea might take the Olympic Games in Tokyo as an opportunity to improve relations with Japan, as it did with

South Korea using the PyeongChang Winter Olympic Games. Japan will respond positively in order to keep North Korea quiet while Japan hosting the Olympic Games, but substantial improvement will not be possible unless North Korea takes meaningful steps towards denuclearization.

Q. The relationship between South Korea and Japan is very bad. Where are we going?

A. We talk about "History issues", but they have become highly politicized. Not many politicians on either side can take a risk and argue how important the bilateral relationship is in the face of mounting anti-Japanese sentiment in Korea and anti-Korea sentiment in Japan. Unfortunately, there seems no good way out at this point. We will probably end up hurting each other, start feeling pain, and eventually realize how important Korea is for Japan and Japan is for Korea. Hopefully, we will start mending fences then.

Q. What should we do then?

A. From the strategic standpoint, it is easy to show how important the bilateral relationship is. International relations textbooks say that nations must balance against rising powers to prevent them from dominating their neighbors. Nations bandwagon with rising powers only if there is no other option. Bandwagoning is a dangerous option with which you sacrifice your sovereignty for security. So, naturally, South Korea, Japan, Australia, Southeast Asian countries, and India must work together to maintain balance here. That's what the textbook says and what Japan is doing today.

Among these countries, South Korea is a critical factor. According to SI-

PRI, South Korea was the tenth largest spender on defense in 2018 with $43.1 billion, and its defense expenditure had increased by 28 percent in the past 10 years. Japan was in ninth place with $46.6 billion spent on defense in 2018. South Korea has a tremendous strategic weight in the region. I sincerely hope that South Korea will find a good balance between cooperating and competing with China going forward as Japan has been trying to do.

Published date: 2019. 08. 20

[VIEW]

Suggestion for restoring Korean-Japanese relations: Agreeing to disagree

By Song Wha-sup, Senior Research Fellow,
Korea Institute for Defense Analyses.

Today, Korean-Japanese relations are going through a turbulent period. Efforts to analyze the reasons behind the strained relationship case by case would be futile because agreement would be difficult.

Instead, now is the time for us to reflect on the bilateral history together to diagnose why we are in a constant state of conflict and seek long-term plans for reconciliation and cooperation.

There are a couple of characteristics when it comes to the bilateral relationship between the countries. First, we assume we are familiar with one another when in fact we lack deeper mutual understanding. Second, we do not recognize the "Difference" between the two when it is perfectly natural for Korea and Japan to be different.

The Koreans easily ask, "What is going on with Japan these days?" whenever some international issues occur between Korea and Japan.

They are led to the notion that it is because Japanese society as a whole is being radicalized. The Japanese, on their part, also ask, "What is going on with Korea these days?" when faced with the same situation.

Korea and Japan are similar in the way that we both achieved substantial economic development and established democracies in the East Asian region. We also share common values such as freedom, democracy, rule of law and human rights. Due to these similarities, however, we easily expect that the other will react in a similar way to a common issue.

But Koreans and Japanese can come to different conclusions because they are different. However, the emphasis should be on the fact that one should be able to understand the other despite the different conclusions drawn. Once we expect the other party to act in accordance with us based on the assumption that we are alike, we are prone to be disappointed and that could easily change to having a negative impression of the other, or even to being angry.

Anti-Japanese sentiment in Korea and anti-Korean sentiment in Japan arise from this context. For example, the anti-Japanese sentiment is based on the thought that Japan lacks adequate historical awareness. The idea, when analyzed more comprehensively, is due to sentiment from the Koreans that Japan, the colonizer, did not repent enough and yet lacks the understanding of the colonized by Korean standards.

On the other hand, the Japanese expect Koreans to perceive and act according to Japanese standards and rationale. They are quick to condemn Korea and ponder anti-Korean sentiment when Koreans deviate from

Japanese expectations.

Such mutual disappointment, based on the mutual similarities, is also apparent in resolving the North Korean nuclear issue. Both countries have shared a common recognition of the problem and have strengthened bilateral security cooperation against military threats from North Korea. However, when it comes to tackling the nuclear issue, Korea hopes to resolve it through dialogue while Japan hopes to pressure North Korea to denuclearize. Under such circumstances, Korea feels regret toward Japan for not joining forces in this endeavor for denuclearization and such feeling is rooted in the said false premise of mutual similarities.

The same applies to the respective policies toward China. Both countries share understanding regarding Chinese military threats. However, they are at odds at how to address the issue.

Japan emphasizes security and military cooperation between Korea and Japan as well as Japan-Korea-U.S. trilateral cooperation. Korea is rather passive when it comes to security cooperation with the international partners targeting China, to avoid any direct conflicts with its northern neighbor. Instead, Korea prefers to remedy military threats through further exchanges and cooperation.

Again, Japan fails to understand the position Korea is taking and argues that Korea is prioritizing China even though Korea is merely demonstrating the "Difference" after considering its respective security concerns.

The Chinese-Japanese relationship has been improving since last year.

Even though Japan is still being menaced by Chinese military threats, it has drifted to the notion of ameliorating bilateral relations through cooperating with China as well as keeping China in check. As such, maritime and aerial communication mechanisms have been established between the two and they are pushing for additional endeavors to prevent accidental clashes.

Changes in the Japanese approach allow room for mutual grounds between Korea and Japan in responding to China. The improvement of Chinese-Japanese relations will guide us to broader trilateral cooperation among Korea, Japan and China. And I sincerely hope that the chance of future trilateral cooperation will be the small stepping stone to reconciliation between Korea and Japan and even to peaceful cooperation for Northeast Asia.

Published date: 2019. 06. 01

[INTERVIEW]

Stopping Korean-Japanese relations drifting further apart

With Nishino Junya, Professor, Keio University.

By Jaeho Hwang

Relations between Korea and Japan seem to be close and distant at the same time, especially these days. There have always been difficulties between the two, but since the beginning of the Abe administration in 2012, relations are going through their toughest and coldest time yet. Bilateral exchanges between the governments have been limited and sporadic while civil exchanges have felt pressured to shy away from the spotlight.

To discuss the past, present and future of this complicated relationship, I sat down with Professor Nishino Junya of Keio University, the director of the Center for Contemporary Korean Studies. Throughout the interview, Professor Nishino shared his honest views on issues surrounding the recent development of Korean-Japanese relations.

Q. How would you evaluate Korean-Japanese relations?

A. There have been issues surrounding history in the past, but they have been managed with mutual consensus to prevent the worst-case scenario. However, the current Japanese government and the influencers think that

"Korea cannot be trusted any longer". And it is not only because of the court ruling on Japanese "Comfort women" compensation but also the recent controversy regarding the radar issues between the two militaries. There has been some disappointment surrounding Korea's argument that blurs the focus of the discussion by focusing on the close-proximity flight issue.

Q. There has been an increase in the possibility of Japanese retaliation after the Supreme Court ruling regarding forced labor.

A. If the plaintiffs request measures to liquidate the assets of the foreclosed Japanese businesses, they will suffer visible damages. Then, it would be very hard for the Japanese government not to do anything about it.

Q. How does the current conflict between the two states differ from the existing conflicts surrounding history?

A. The difference is that the ongoing conflict is the by-product of a structure that was constructed through the qualitative changes and the different perspectives in the international community of the two states. During the Cold War and before the democratization of Korea, Korean-Japanese relations were limited to political-diplomatic matters, making them easier to manage. However, today they have become highly complicated due to the inclusion of civil societies. The involvement of civil societies is positive in that it stimulates exchanges between the citizens, but it also makes it easier for the relations to be volatile, by making the governments swayed by public opinion or public sentiment. Also, there is a fundamental difference between Korea and Japan when it comes to how to accept and react to the grand changes — that is the rise of China, as we have seen former President Park Geun-hye on the Tiananmen Square watchtower. This difference works as the driving force for increasing the distance between Korea and Japan.

Q. Are there any political and economic elements to the increasing distance between the two?

A. Korea became proud as one of the influential states in the international community due to economic growth. Japan, on the other hand, has lost its confidence after the long depression called the "Lost 20 years" and in 2011 the Great East Japan Earthquake. The economic and military rise of China in the 2010s also is a factor that makes Japan less confident. The Abe administration succeeded in getting a second term by taking advantage of this situation. The changes in the psyches of Koreans and Japanese led to the changes in bilateral relations. The intense conflict between progressives and conservatives in Korean politics is one of the elements negatively affecting Korean-Japanese relations. The ideological conflict often leads to the historical disputes about the basis for the legitimacy of Korea, affecting the relationship between the two countries.

Q. A few weeks ago, Kim Jong-un met President Vladimir Putin in a North Korea-Russia Summit. Kim has met all the leaders from South Korea, the U.S., China and Russia, with Prime Minister Abe remaining.

A. Prime Minister Abe has repeatedly said he is ready to meet Chairman Kim since last summer. However, there is a condition for the North Korea-Japan Summit to take place. That is, the summit itself should contribute to the resolution of the Japanese abductees issue that concerns both parties. If Kim demonstrates a sincere willingness to resolve the abductee issue to push for any progress in North Korea-Japan relations with a long-term perspective, then a Kim-Abe summit can happen any time.

The normalization of North Korea-Japan relations will bring the Japanese economic aid necessary to boost the North Korean economy.

Q. There has been the ascension of a new emperor in May and there also will be a G20 summit in Osaka. Could these two events improve Korea-Japan relations?

A. I hope there will be a Korea-Japan summit on the sidelines of the G20 meeting, but it will be hard to achieve any tangible outcome. There is a chance of talks between Moon and Abe backfiring by demonstrating the different perspectives between the two. Therefore, we need to be cautious.

Q. Are there any additional comments on the future development of Korea-Japan relations?

A. After the 2010s, the structural changes that both of our countries face, such as social changes and changes in the international order in East Asia, call for "New Korea-Japan relations". The situation today clearly demonstrates the limitations of the contribution from the active civil societies in maintaining the healthy bilateral relationship. We — both the citizens and the political leaders — need to manage the current transition period and to recognize and firmly believe in the vision that we are building a new relationship.

Published date: 2019. 05. 04

2. 4. South Korea and Neighbors

[INTERVIEW]

India closer to Korea than you think in diplomatic and security policy

With Vinod Anand, Senior Fellow, Vivekananda International Foundation (VIF), New Delhi.
By Jaeho Hwang

One of the most notable traits of the current Moon administration in terms of diplomatic policy is the strengthening of relations with India. The sense of sympathy and active interaction between President Moon Jae-in and Prime Minister Narendra Modi make us feel that Korea and India are closer than ever. Indeed, India's support for Korea's plans and policies regarding peace building and stability on the Korean Peninsula is a source of great strength for Korea.

However, it is not widely known domestically how India is promoting its own diplomatic, security and defense policies. To seek an answer to our query, Professor Jaeho Hwang of Hankuk University of Foreign Studies sat down with Vinod Anand, a Senior Fellow at the Vivekananda International Foundation (VIF), visiting Korea for the 2019 Korea Foundation Invitation Program for Distinguished Guests in Foreign Policies and Security, in the second week of April.

Q. What is the purpose of your visit to Korea?

A. The aim of my visit to South Korea was to interact and engage with scholars and experts from think tanks and the strategic community and also government officials to better understand South Korea's foreign and security policies. The interactions at the Korea Foundation, Ministry of Foreign Affairs, Korean National Diplomatic Academy and Korean Institute of Defense Analyses provided me with better insights into the South Korean perspective on a variety of strategic and security issues.

Q. What is the priority of the Indian security policy?

A. The main objective of India's security policies is to support peace and stability efforts in the region and world at large in order to enhance prosperity and economic growth. In terms of security threats and challenges, dealing with terrorism remains the top priority. India has been facing the scourge of terrorism from across its borders since almost its inception in 1947. Further, India has a tough neighborhood wherein its borders with nuclearized China and Pakistan remain unsettled. While there is firing across the Line of Control between India and Pakistan almost on a daily basis, not a single shot has been fired on the Line of Actual Control between India and China since 1986.

Q. How is the modernization of Indian defense forces progressing?

A. The modernization of Indian defense forces is progressing at a steady pace. Though there is a need to increase the defense budget, the government has to be judicious in allotting funds to other competing sectors, e.g. health, education and many other infrastructure and developmental plans. However, the government is paying particular attention to the development of the indigenous defense industry and transfer of technology from abroad. While India has been importing a variety of defense weapons and systems from abroad, it has also gone in a big way for the "Make in India" program. There are a number of areas where both India and South Korea can cooperate in defense manufacturing for mutual benefit. India has good capabilities in space, cyber and special forces operations; cooperation between both sides would result in exploiting the synergies. Over the year, Indian armed forces have modernized their doctrinal concepts and precepts and also added to their deterrent capabilities with a view to meeting the challenges from potential adversaries.

Q. How would you evaluate India's Act East Policy?

A. Since the unveiling of India's Look East Policy in 1992 and now its transformation to the Act East Policy in November 2014, it has undergone many iterations. While the original objective of the policy was to reintegrate with the neighborhood and extended neighborhood through a variety of connectivity efforts and economic initiatives, the policy has now acquired a certain degree of strategic orientation. The Act East Policy also chimes very well with South Korea's New Southern Policy, which was ushered in by President Moon Jae-in. Thus, South Korea's efforts to reach out to ASEAN and beyond to India and South Asia complement New Delhi's objectives of strengthening relationships with ASEAN and East Asian nations. It can be easily said that India has been able to achieve a considerable degree of success in its engagement with ASEAN, South Korea and Japan. The Act East Policy also pre-dates many of the other connectivity and other initiatives in the region. Thus, it cannot be said that India's Act East Policy is counter to or in response to any other policy initiatives promoted by other countries in the region.

Q. What is India's China policy?

A. As mentioned earlier, India and China have a disputed border and even mutual perceptions as to where the Line of Actual Control (LAC) lies differ. Thus, there is always a potential for a conflict that could go out of control. However, India's policy is to maintain peace and tranquility along the LAC and urge China to at least agree to a shared perception of the LAC, even if the boundary agreement cannot be reached in an earlier timeframe. The Doklam incident along the India-China border in August 2017, where troops from both sides faced each other for 73 days or so, was symptomatic of the possibilities of a hot conflict. Indian forces stood their ground, which later led to the Wuhan meeting and a degree of consensus between both sides.

Further, India's approach is to develop itself economically while putting the differences with China aside. As India has been running a huge deficit of around $60 billion (2018) with China, New Delhi has been urging China to address the trade deficit through the opening up of its markets and removing certain non-tariff trade barriers. There is a wide degree of acceptance by both sides that they cannot afford any conflict as it would not benefit any side.

Q. What is India's position toward the One Belt, One Road Initiative?

A. India's objections to the Belt and Road Initiative (BRI) mainly arise from China building its China-Pakistan Economic Corridor that passes through Indian territory occupied by Pakistan. Indian leadership has articulated its position at many forums that connectivity projects must be pursued in a manner that respects sovereignty and territorial integrity. On the other hand, one of the basic tenets of India's current policy toward

China has been to utilize Chinese capabilities to advance India's developmental agenda. India needs a massive amount of funds for its infrastructure projects. India became a member of the Asian Infrastructure Investment Bank and the New Development Bank of BRICS to utilize such opportunities for accessing development funds. India has no objections to China undertaking infrastructure and other developmental projects in India, subject to international norms and mutual agreement on terms and conditions but without being under the overarching ambit of the BRI.

Q. How do you see current Korean-Indian relations?

A. With President Moon Jae-in's visit to India in July 2018 and PM Narendra Modi's visit to South Korea in February this year, bilateral relations have gained considerable momentum. President Moon, after coming to power in 2017, has paid particular attention to boosting the relationship with India, which is also reflected in sending a Special Envoy to India for the first time. Earlier in 2015, during PM Modi's visit to Seoul, the existing Strategic Partnership between the two countries, which is based on shared values and interests, was upgraded to the Special Strategic Partnership. Many South Korean brands like Samsung, Hyundai, LG, etc., are household names in India. Though bilateral trade has stagnated around $20 billion for some years, there are plans to increase trade to $50 billion by 2030. For this reason, the Comprehensive Economic Partnership Agreement is being reviewed by both sides. India views South Korea as an important partner in India's economic transformation.

Q. Are there any additional comments?

A. In addition to developing a strong economic relationship, there is also a need to enhance defense and security ties. Meanwhile, boosting the people-to-people relationship also remains equally important.

Published date: 2019. 04. 27

[INTERVIEW]

Is India leaning toward the fifth axis of South Korea's diplomacy?

With Dhruva Jaishankar, Fellow, Brookings India, New Delhi.

By Jaeho Hwang

For Korea, India carries a mystic image. Known for the first international marriage in our history, a princess from an ancient kingdom in Ayodhya, India, became the queen of Korea's Gaya Kingdom about 2,000 years ago.

India, with a colonial past like Korea, was a leader of Third World, non-aligned countries during the Cold War. Though psychologically close, there were never enough links to further develop relations between the two countries. It is true that India was on the outskirts of South Korea's foreign security environment, which was occupied by the absolute conditions of the U.S., China, Japan and Russia.

However, with the arrival of Moon Jae-In's government, India's importance in South Korea's foreign policy has greatly increased. One of the key foreign policies for the Moon administration, the New Southern Policy, is an effort to raise Korea-India relations to the level of the four-way diplomacy with the U.S., China, Japan and Russia, which is the core of

Korean diplomacy. Meanwhile, it is a positive affirmation in terms of a change in perception to move beyond our four-way diplomacy as well as an attempt to reduce the heavy reliance on these public economies.

South Korean President Moon Jae-in made a state visit to India from July 8 to 11 and held a summit with Indian Prime Minister Narendra Modi to discuss strategies on the expansion of future-oriented cooperation. It is likely India's importance will continue to grow.

For an overview of the present and future of Korea-India relations, here is an interview with Indian foreign policy expert Dhruva Jaishankar. He is a Fellow of Foreign Policy, at Brookings India in New Delhi and the Brookings Institution in Washington, D.C. He is also a non-resident fellow with the Lowy Institute in Australia. He was previously a fellow at the German Marshall Fund in Washington and at the S. Rajaratnam School of International Studies in Singapore. He was educated at Macalester College and Georgetown University.

Q. How would you sum up the Indian foreign policy?

A. It is hard to sum up India's complex foreign engagements in a few words, but most of India's objectives can be placed in five broad categories. One: Using foreign policy to accelerate India's domestic development, including through sourcing investment and technology, improved standards, diaspora outreach, security cooperation, and other means. Two: Maintaining a stable periphery by improving neighbourhood connectivity and regional integration. For a variety of reasons, this process is often frustrating. Three: India's Act East Policy is meant to preserve a favorable balance of power in the Indo-Pacific region in light of China's rise. A fourth goal is countering terrorism and instability to India's west, including through some difficult diplomacy with Pakistan and efforts to stabilize Afghanistan. And five, creating space in forums of global governance so that India's interests can be adequately represented on such issues as climate change, monetary coordination, institutional lending, international security and nuclear non-proliferation. This extends to involvement at such institutions as the United Nations, the G20, the East Asia Summit and the Asian Infrastructure Investment Bank (AIIB).

Q. How do you evaluate India-China relations?

A. India-China relations are complex but consist of four defining elements. Two have traditionally been contentious. On bilateral security, the two countries have a long-standing boundary dispute, and we have witnessed occasional military standoffs along the border. Second, on regional security, India has always had concerns about Chinese influence in its near abroad and the Indian Ocean region, and these have only increased with the Belt and Road Initiative (BRI). India has boycotted BRI, which it sees as traversing territory disputed between India and Pakistan and thus an affront to its sovereignty. More importantly, India sees China's BRI financing as unsustainable, creating conditions for debt to be leveraged for strategic purposes.

Two other areas of India-China relations have traditionally been more cooperative. Bilateral trade and economic relations have improved significantly since 2000, but the trade deficit has widened in China's favor, and Indian businesses are increasingly frustrated with the lack of market opportunities there.

On global governance, India and China traditionally cooperated on various issues such as climate change and at the U.N., BRICS and the AIIB, but there have been growing differences, in part due to China's self-perception as a power on par with the United States. China has thus not supported India's membership at the U.N. Security Council and the Nuclear Suppliers Group. Consequently, all four elements of India-China relations have become more difficult over the past five years or so. While this year has seen some tactical efforts at managing differences, the longer-run trends suggest a much more competitive and contentious relationship between two countries with billion-plus populations.

Q. Do you consider the Indo-Pacific strategy substantial?

A. The Indo-Pacific has entered the official strategic vocabulary of several countries — including India — in recent years. Essentially, it implies at least three things: that the Indian and Pacific oceans are part of a single strategic space; that the maritime domain is strategically and economically significant, and (indirectly) that India plays an important role in the regional balance of power as the largest economy and military in the Indian Ocean region. These are the common strands to the use of the term Indo-Pacific by India, the United States, Japan, Australia, and others. However, while the United States and Japan have their own "Free and open Indo-Pacific" strategies, India views the Indo-Pacific not as a strategy, but as a space in which its Act East Policy will be implemented.

In essence, this means securing the Indian Ocean, deepening connectivity with Southeast Asia, improving security partnerships with the United States, Japan and others who have shared concerns about China's rise, and managing an increasingly difficult relationship with Beijing. To this extent, the Indian Navy and Indian aid have been playing a more active role in the Indian Ocean, India has increased its diplomatic activity and security relations with ASEAN (including hosting all 10 leaders in Delhi this year), and has also made headway with the United States, Japan, and Australia. If there is a weakness, it has been in India's insufficient economic integration with the region as a whole.

Q. What do you think of Korea's New Southern Policy?

A. South Korea has for many years punched above its weight on economic matters and has a potent military. However, it has been preoccupied with strategic concerns on the Korean Peninsula, resulting in a bit of a mismatch between its capabilities and its influence in the broader region. Insofar as the New Southern Policy marks a willingness to engage strategically with that wider region, it is a very welcome sign. President Moon Jae-In's visit to India earlier this year was a step in the right direction.

Q. Would you share your thoughts on the current situation on the Korean Peninsula, including the denuclearization?

A. I'm no expert on Korean Peninsula issues, but have naturally been following developments there for many years. India had historically played a very active role on the Korean Peninsula, including through the provision of military aid during the Korean War under a United Nations banner and in the repatriation of prisoners of war in the 1950s. India has since maintained diplomatic ties with both Seoul and Pyongyang, although economically, politically and in terms of values, India shares much more in common with the Republic of Korea than with the DPRK.

Recently, while welcoming diplomatic efforts between the two sides, New Delhi has become more overtly critical of the North's development of nuclear and missile technology and has participated in international sanctions against Pyongyang.

Q. Please suggest the direction for India-Korea relations to be developed to another level.

A. Economically, relations are quite strong. Korean companies have performed well in the Indian market and a Comprehensive Economic Partnership Agreement (CEPA) was signed in 2009, although trade could still improve. In terms of security, relations have been taking off from a relatively low base. The fact that Korea was one of the first overseas destinations of the previous Indian defence minister is indicative of that fact. Two areas, however, are deserving of much greater attention. One is improving people-to-people ties and contacts. This would mean increasing the incentives and opportunities for the exchange of tourists, students, businesspeople and other visitors. Two, there is scope for improving the strategic component of the relationship by sharing lessons learned. After all, both India and the Republic of Korea are involved in difficult negotiations with nuclear-armed neighbors whose leaderships are not always interested in engagement. Yet there have been few efforts by New Delhi and Seoul to systematically learn from each other's experiences. In these domains, India-Korea relations stand to improve tremendously.

To conclude, President Moon showed intimacy with Indian Prime Minister Modi as they were even seen together riding the New Delhi subway during Moon's state visit in July. As mentioned in his speech at the Korea-India Business Forum: "Many Indian people drive Hyundai cars and use Samsung mobile phones while many people in Korea enjoy curry and practice yoga. No need to look far for an example, my daughter teaches yoga in Korea".

Whether the relationship of the two countries' leaders and the people will lean toward India as the next South Korean axis in foreign policies must be observed through the development of South Korea's New Southern Policy within the remaining four years of the Moon administration.

Published date: 2018. 08. 25

[INTERVIEW]

Park Hang-seo's magical effect on ROK-Vietnam relations

With Julia Luong Dinh, Senior Research Fellow, Diplomatic Academy of Vietnam.
By Jaeho Hwang

Who might be the most famous Korean to the 100 million Vietnamese these days? The answer is definitely Park Hang-seo, coach of Vietnam's U-23 national football team. He has realized the dream of Vietnam by leading the team to the first semi-final at the Asian Games 2018.

In January, after only three months in the job, he led the team to the first semi-final match in the Asia Football Confederation U-23 Championship. This was not only a step forward for Vietnam, but also for all Southeast Asian countries. Due to Park's impressive performance, Vietnam's Prime Minister Nguyen Xuan Phuc invited Park and his team to his place on Vietnam's National Day.

By virtue of Park's record, Koreans also started being interested in Vietnam. Before, when thinking of Vietnam, Korea rather was more familiar with the image of a naked child running away from soldiers in the Vietnam War. But Vietnam is now considered the biggest and representative Southeast Asian country with a potential for development. In addition, it is one of the core countries of President Moon Jae-in's New Southern Policy.

In fact, Vietnam has several things in common with Korea. Vietnam has gone through national division and has fought against the major powers to gain its independence. Korea and Vietnam also were in the same boat in the sense of international politics that they had to combat during the Cold War. Seeing through the common flows, it would be interesting to look into Vietnam's security conditions and its diplomatic strategy. What will Vietnam's new circumstances be while it strives to build the New Vietnam through reform and opening? We invited Dr. Julia Luong Dinh from the Diplomatic Academy of Vietnam to shed some light on these and other issues.

Dr. Julia Luong Dinh is a Senior research fellow at the Institute of Foreign Policy and Strategic Studies, Diplomatic Academy of Vietnam (DAV), and a lecturer in the Joint Training Programme between DAV and Victoria University of Wellington (New Zealand). Dr. Dinh got her Doctoral Degree from the University of Sydney. Her research background and interests are Chinese foreign policy, power politics, regionalism, international relation theory and practice in East Asia.

Q. What is the strong point/forte of Vietnamese foreign policy?

A. Built upon a time-honored diplomacy, Vietnamese foreign policy reflects centuries of diplomatic practice and aims to maintain a peaceful and stable environment for national development in a globalized world. A consistent foreign policy of self-reliance, independence, peace and cooperation under the leadership of state and government has effectively contributed to Vietnam's international integration, thus enhancing Vietnam's international status in a new situation. Currently, Vietnam boasts of a positive relationship with all five members in the UNSC, all leading industrial nations in the G7, 13 out of G20 member countries, worldwide networking with 27 strategic/comprehensive strategic partnerships and 12 new-generation FTAs (10 FTAs in effect), etc.

Q. How do you evaluate the Chinese foreign policy?

A. It is never an easy task to discuss China, and it is even more difficult to fully evaluate Chinese foreign policy in a rapidly changing world featured by uncertainties in these days. On the one hand, I believe that Chinese people are great in many ways, and China has all it needs to materialize its long-awaited rejuvenation as a great nation. As a big country, the Chinese government has quite a few policy instruments and strategies to pursue their goals and targets set on its ambitious agenda. At home, President Xi himself has, by the 19th Party Congress, consolidated his power and championed the domestic consensus in accelerating China's foreign policy and a global agenda thanks to the myth and pledge that the ruling Communist Party of China (CPC) under his paramount leadership is the only solution to China's problems. Internationally, China's "Check diplomacy", coupled with its robust military, especially in its navy build-up in strategic waters, has garnered Beijing less trust than fear from its neighbors and partners near and far.

On the other hand, Beijing leaders, however, should be more aware of the fact that the utilization of power and resources has become increasingly "Unconventional" in a rapidly changing world with "Unconventional" practice and policy practitioners. China is facing the most crucial challenge to re-assert its position on the global stage both from within and from without. A long standoff with President Trump over trade would irresistibly result in CPC's tainted image and poor merits in governance, revealing the Achilles heel of China's economic structure/model and President's Xi failed commitments to sustain economic growth for China.

Q. How are current China-Vietnam relations?

A. From my own perspective, the current bilateral relations have left much to be desired given a number of untapped potentials. The consensus made among the high-ranking leaders and policy implementation have hardly dismissed the simmering grievances at the grassroots level. Lack of mutual trust in security and defense areas has been exacerbated by the ongoing strategic rivalry among regional powers. However, China and Vietnam have momentums to gain a substantive breakthrough in bilateral cooperation and envision an upward trajectory of the relations. Big powers like China have a bigger role and more policy instruments than the smaller one in determining the future course of this asymmetric relationship, especially in constructively resolving existing disputes between two sides. For its part, Vietnam should address concerns in relations with China from a strategic approach to pave the way for an inclusive and beneficial cooperation with the world's second-largest economy.

Q. What is the Vietnamese perspective/view on South Korea?

A. First, South Korea is a medium power in the Northeast Asia region. Assiduous efforts by South Korea to set in motion the initial steps of easing tension and hostilities, facilitating the reconciliation process on the Korean Peninsula, are remarkable contributions to regional peace and stability. Second, South Korean companies' investments in Vietnam are expected to play an active role in bringing in the latter's sustainable development and the win-win fruits for both sides against the tide of protectionism and anti-globalization, serving as a good example of bilateral cooperation amidst a slowdown in regional and multilateral trading arrangements. Third, Vietnam and South Korea have undergone thick and thin throughout history, sharing many commonalities in traditional culture, norms and values. The Vietnamese government and people highly value and treasure good neighborliness with South Korea.

Q. Since South Korea stands between the alliance with the U.S. and partnership with China, South Korea has lots of concerns. Where does Vietnam stand between the U.S. and China?

A. As I mentioned above, geopolitics and strategic rivalries among big powers do more harm to small countries. As a small country which long experienced power politics before and during the Cold War, Vietnam's consistent policy is to befriend all countries, not taking sides or going with any country against the third country. Vietnam is committed to persistently safeguarding national independence, sovereignty and legitimate interests in line with international law, and resolutely opposing any attempts to intervene in our internal affairs.

In short, the Korean media refers to Park Hang-seo's magic as the trend these days, however, I am looking forward to see Vietnam's magic. Once the Doi Moi Reform and Opening succeeds, it will become a development model. China's development model, which aims for 1.4billion people, might not be appropriate for small countries with less population. Furthermore, a confident and practical diplomacy will come along with magical effects. We are now anticipating what it will bring to the ROK-Vietnam relations.

Published date: 2018. 09. 08

2. 5. North Korea and Neighbors

[REVIEW]

North Korea conundrum

By Yang Un-chul, Senior Research Fellow,
Sejong Institute.

Since the historical summits between the two Koreas and the U.S. and North Korea, the international community's interest mainly focuses on the denuclearization of North Korea and its consequences. However, North Korea has continued to strengthen its traditional military capabilities with nuclear development over the past 20 years.

It is believed that North Korea has pursued changes in military structure and strategy based on its own circumstances due to its poor economic reality. Evidently, North Korea has shown clear signs of strengthening asymmetric power in terms of weapons of mass destruction, including nuclear and chemical weapons, missiles and conventional forces, such as the special force and submarines, since the 1990s. Recently, it was revealed that North Korea's asymmetric power buildup has been developing into new aspects such as cyber warfare, electronic warfare and unmanned aerial vehicles.

In this situation, denuclearization of North Korea, which the world is paying attention to, has not found a solution. Fundamentally, the national interests of North Korea and the U.S. are different from the way they are solved. The United States is pleased with the role of the international community in the ongoing economic sanctions, but North Korea has identified the sanctions as the biggest barrier to denuclearization.

Regardless of denuclearization, it is anticipated that pressure by the international community will continue over issues such as the violation of human rights, cyber terror, and so on. That puts substantial pressure on North Korea.

In the diplomatic perspective, it is hard to expect North Korea's relations with China to be restored as a full alliance. North Korea may have doubts about the authenticity of China's active participation in economic sanctions against it, but it believes China does not give North Korea enough support.

Pyongyang is always concerned about China's growing influence over the country. Under such circumstances, North Korea must enter a normal state through continuous reforms. North Korea's true leap forward will come when it joins the international economic organization, and eventually North Korea will be transformed into a normal state.

North Korea's conventional weapons, stagnant economy, cyber terrorism and accession to international organizations are difficult problems to solve in the short term. If these difficulties are not resolved, even if North Korea's denuclearization is achieved, it will be difficult for North Korea to change into a normal nation.

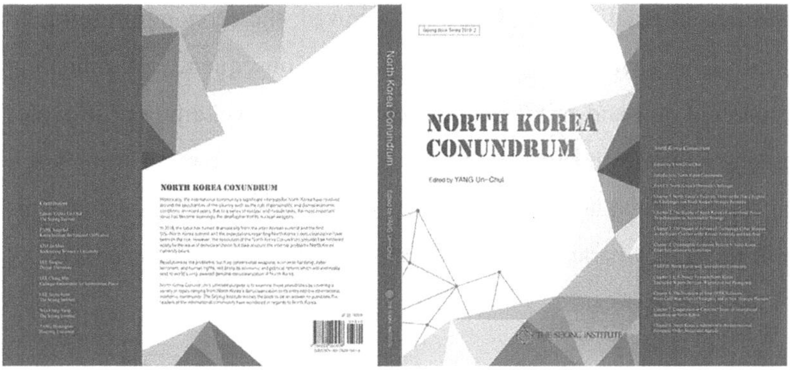

North Korea's internal situation seems hard to fathom when the nuclear issue is an international issue. North Korea's official economy intends to increase the mobilization of internal resources. And its foreign currency earning business has reached its limit due to the economic sanctions. For that, Kim Jong-un is driving North Koreans to desperation to obedience. However, the economic performance is less than expected. On the other hand, the private market has grown rapidly.

As history bears witness, a market evolves against all odds. The pressure from the bottom of society to provide reform measures continues to increase as the capacity of the North Korean regime decreases. With the slow paradigm shift of North Korean people and the elites, the foundation to implement a market economy will certainly spread economic rent to the people. At the same time, Kim is providing economic rent to his followers as he progresses North Korean economic reforms, such as reforming the corporate law, allowing market activities and localization by substituting imports.

However, if economic freedoms such as individual property ownership and free international trade are not allowed, the economic reforms in North Korea will have a negative effect. Consequently, diminishing economic rent and privileges will eventually provoke power struggles among Kim's core supporting groups to obtain more rent. Then, North Korea's political and military power will weaken in the long run. This will be the key parameter that determines Kim Jong-un's power stability in the near future.

The book "North Korea Conundrum" is designed with the intention of analyzing the problems and constraints of these North Korean's conundrums. If North Korea solves the problems — including denuclearization — one by one, the true prosperity of North Korea will be possible. This book discusses the essential possibility of solving the North Korean problem by addressing various issues, ranging from denuclearization of North Korea to joining the world economic system. We expect this book will answer the questions the international community has about North Korea and provide clues to resolve North Korea's difficult problems. In addition, this book will help us break out of the trap of prevailing notions and conventional wisdom that have occasionally perverted our perceptions of North Korea.

Published date: 2019. 04. 20

[VIEW]

How North Korea can use auctions and radical markets to foster growth and governance

By Jasper Kim, Professor, Ewha Womans University.

In the recent Trump-Kim summits, both world leaders expressed hope based in part on a "Mutual gains" model. Such a model is predicated on a "Win-win", where both sides can come out better ahead. Such a successful outcome is seemingly predicated, at least in part, on economic development utilizing aspects of free market principles, such as foreign investment and even real estate development.

North Korea today, unbeknown to many, exercises some level of free market capitalism today. Most don't think or hear about free markets in the DPRK, mainly because, when it comes to regular citizens, such activity has largely been rendered less than free and deemed illegal, thus largely relegated to an underground economy. At the macro-level, North Korea has already implemented several free economic zones to incentivize foreign investment, which in itself constitutes a derivative form of free market capitalism.

But suppose that the DPRK does decide to further, rather than dampen, free market capitalism in its own interpretation and perception, similar to the economic growth stories of Vietnam and China. And suppose that as its economy begins to strengthen, how should the state trust its citizens to pay their "Fair" share of taxes? Conversely, how would the people trust its government that such collected funds (taxes) were being used properly and for the greater good of the people?

Taxes represent an important revenue source for many economies. And as individual and corporate tax rates gather steam, so would government revenue. The issue then becomes how to assess and collect taxes with minimal administrative burden while securing the "Greatest good" for both the people and state.

If the people do not trust the state with this objective, then tax avoidance (where taxpayers attempt to minimize tax payments) or even tax evasion (where taxpayers do not pay owed obligations) may occur, by which the state would not benefit. In economic parlance, this would be a non-Pareto outcome, which, in plain language, simply means that more tax revenue could have been collected if greater trust in the tax system existed.

One possible solution may come from "Radical Markets". This is a concept based on a recent book by two economists, Eric Posner (University of Chicago) and E. Glen Weyl (Microsoft).

Posner and Weyl propose a radically different approach to taxation and governance that may appeal to capitalists, socialists and Stalinists (DPRK) alike: "Imagine a world in which all major private wealth (every factory, patent or plot of land) is constantly for sale at a fair price and where most of the value of this property is paid out equally to all citizens as a social dividend. "While one might be tempted to believe the wealthy would dominate such a hyper-market world, in fact most private wealth would become social wealth and would be shared equally by all. With most value of assets accruing to the public, every asset would become cheaper to (partially) own, democratizing the control of assets and offering everyone new opportunities to start businesses or households. At the same time, because there would be a price on every asset, large-scale projects, like high-speed trains, would become far easier to develop as holdouts could no longer block the right of way".

To implement such grand new deal, they propose a new property system, called the Common Ownership Self-Assessed Tax (COST). In the newly devised COST system, every person or entity (corporation, non-profit, etc) would "Self-assess" the value of their owned assets and pay about a seven percent tax on those self-assessed values.

All such owned assets would be required to be sold to any buyer willing to purchase such assets at such self-assessed price — a type of auction system — whereby all private property would be listed and viewable (say, via an online registry viewable by all, in the spirit of total transparency).

Because of this auction-style feature, owners would be greatly incentivized to assess the true "Fair" value of their owned assets. After all, if the owner sets too low a price to lower her taxes, then that would increase the chance of a party buying that asset since it would seem like a good deal (relative to other similar products/services). On the other hand, if the owner sets too high a price to keep the asset out of the hands of would-be buyers, then that would lead to greater taxes assessed for that owner.

The tax revenue raised should be sufficient to "Repeal and replace" other taxes on capital (such as corporation tax, capital gains tax, property tax and inheritance tax), while "Significantly reducing" personal income taxes. Such collected tax revenues would also help in paying down public (state) debt.

The proceeds of such collected "Auction-style" self-assessed tax revenue by the state would be returned to the people in the form of a "Large social dividend" — a form of universal basic income (UBI). In the U.S. case, this would amount to about $24,000 for a family of four people (separate from any other income). The remaining funds would be used to subsidize (pay for) free public resources such as public transport, highways and other infrastructure for the 21st century.

The COST auction-style tax system is also estimated to increase the economy by about five percent.

Another added benefit would be a "Healthier relationship" with property. This would be in stark contrast to today's commercial culture, arguably overly predicated on fetishization of ownership of non-necessities, such as luxury goods and conspicuous consumption to signal wealth (a form of "Keeping up with the Joneses", a hamster wheel-type phenomenon whereby something is never enough).

Other advantages include a shared goal of increasing the value of the wealth of a nation while strengthening community bonds.

Given that North Korea's tax base is arguably at a nascent stage, the cost-benefit analysis may tilt now or later toward implementation of this bold approach, in whole or part, for greater tax revenue, trust and transparency that both the people and the state would consider a "Mutual gain" and a "Win-win".

The "Radical Markets" system may appear unorthodox now — but so too were the original unorthodox ideas of free markets, democracy and the invisible hand when first proffered.

Published date: 2019. 10. 05

[INTERVIEW]

Korean Peninsula peace dream shimmering in front of us

With Dean Ouellette, Vice Director, Institute for Far Eastern Studies, Seoul.

By Jaeho Hwang

The situation on the Korean Peninsula is flowing quite fast. On August 13, there were high-level talks between the two Koreas and a third inter-Korean summit, to be held in September in Pyongyang, was recently announced. President Moon Jae-in made the point in his message for the 73rd Korean National Liberation Day that Korea will take another step toward the declaration of the end of the Korean War and a peace treaty.

Since this year's inter-Korean summit and the U.S.-North Korea summit are historically significant as the beginning of the Korean Peninsula's peace, Moon emphasized focusing on peace on the peninsula. In this context, he also brought up how the denuclearization and peace regime would contribute to acceleration of economic cooperation between the two Koreas and eventually achieve common economic prosperity.

Considering the current dynamics on the peninsula, an interview with Dean J. Ouellette was very informative. Ouellette is a renowned Canadian scholar in North Korean studies. He is the vice director/director of international affairs at the Institute for Far Eastern Studies, Kyungnam University, and associate professor at the university's Department of Political Science and Diplomacy. His research interests include North Korea's relations with state and non-state actors, North Korean tourism, and trust-building and peace-building on the Korean Peninsula.

Q. How do you evaluate North Korea's recent attitude?

A. I assume you mean North Korea's shift from obstinacy to outreach. Tensions in the region rose to worrisome levels in 2017 on account of North Korea's ballistic missile and nuclear tests. But leader Kim Jong-un changed tack in early 2018, forgoing provocations in favour of a "Peace" offensive. North Korean athletes and cheering squads were dispatched to the 2018 PyeongChang Winter Olympics. High-level delegations visited South Korea — and surprisingly so did the leader's sister, Kim Yo-jong.

A flurry of diplomatic activity followed, punctuated by Chairman Kim's own international road trips to attend several historic summits that included two meetings with South Korean President Moon Jae-in (in April and May at Panmunjeom), one with US President Donald Trump (in June at Singapore), and three with Chinese President Xi Jinping (in March, May and June in Beijing, Dalian and Beijing, respectively).

With this shift, Kim seems to be signaling peace and a desire for diplomacy. Indeed, facilitating "Close contact and active dialogue with neighbouring countries and the international community" are essential in order to reduce tensions and allow for Kim to succeed in creating a peaceful international environment favorable for North Korea to refocus all efforts toward "Socialist economic construction" — the country's new "Strategic line" that Kim himself announced in mid-April.

Q. Since Kim already has visited China three times in the first half of this year, do you consider China-North Korea relations have been recovered?

A. To some extent, yes. Those meetings between Kim and Xi Jinping, and Xi's expression of satisfaction with Kim's efforts toward denuclearization and focus on economic construction, suggest better times ahead for Sino-DPRK relations. Nevertheless, I still question the strength of the relationship's bonds, and thus the relations in general.

The Kim-family regime's dislike and distrust of its neighbour are no secret — it stretches back in history to the public denunciations of Kim Il-sung by China's radical Red Guards during the Cultural Revolution. Kim Jong-un himself may have his own reasons to be wary of the powerful 60-year-old oligarchs who rule China. Allegations that surfaced imply that China's top men had been approached by Jang Song-thaek (Kim Jong-un's uncle) with a plot to stage a coup against the young leader and then install Kim's estranged half-brother, Kim Jong-nam, as the new sovereign. (Both uncle and half-brother are now dead, one executed in 2013, the other assassinated in 2017.)

Q. How do you see recent South-North Korea relations?

A. Inter-Korean relations are the best they've been in over a decade. The Moon-Kim summit in April 2018 was an historic event. If peace is to come to the Korean Peninsula, the two Koreas must lead that effort. As long as both leaders remain honest, realistic, committed and engaged to that effort, I think we can expect incremental improvements in the relations. However, it is unclear whether North Korea has made the strategic decisions to overcome the critical obstacles — denuclearization, opening and reform. For its part, I believe Seoul must work to maintain the positive momentum toward fostering an environment for Pyongyang to stay engaged, make those strategic decisions and join the international community?

Q. How would you evaluate North Korea's current economic status?

A. The recent Bank of Korea estimate suggests North Korea's GDP shrank by roughly 3.5 percent in 2017. The heavy sanctions against the country no doubt must be negatively impacting the economy, and the trade situation cannot be great. Yet, I speculate that North Korea is not yet in dire straits. For example, some experts point to stable market prices for food so far throughout 2018 as a sign of economic stability — and a plus for the people. As well, economic improvement measures of the recent past, in the form of more enterprise autonomy and incentives for farmers, may also be having limited yet positive effects.

Furthermore, the regime itself continues to work to make ends meet by finding ways to circumvent sanctions, earn foreign exchange and obtain energy sources — as suggested by recent U.N. and other reports detailing illicit ship-to-ship transfers of fuel products, Russia's underreporting of oil deliveries and North Korean labor's return to factories, construction sites and restaurants in China and Russia. To some extent, it seems the hidden valves controlling some of the sanctions pressure have already been turned down a notch, providing North Korea relief.

Q. What do you predict for further inter-Korea economic cooperation?

A. Without serious steps toward denuclearization, it is hard to envision significant inter-Korean economic cooperation really moving forward. Seoul's hands are tied by international sanctions. Most recently, through its media, North Korea is making demands for South Korea to show substantive action to improve inter-Korean relations by not sticking to the long-held "Sanctions and pressure scheme" and instead propelling forward inter-Korean cooperation projects such as modernization of rails and roads in the North and the resumption of Mount Kumgang tourism. At the moment, prospects for such projects look dim.

Q. Which economic sector of North Korea do you consider the most competitive?

A. In the near term, there seem high hopes for the tourism sector. In past eras this sector was necessary but never important. That changed under Kim Jong-un's watch. Tourism (and sport) is part of the marshal's image branding and a noteworthy component of his special economic zones policy. Kim is allocating money and resources into developing select tourism-related infrastructure and manpower, reclassifying military properties (like airports and hotels) in part for civilian/tourism use, and allowing domestic industry professionals to innovate with new products and services, inter alia.

As long as peaceful diplomacy, and not provocations, remains his desire and drive, I suspect he'll continue to have China to tap for tourists — the industry's major market and one North Korea can somewhat reliably count on and control to earn foreign currency. If inter-Korean relations improve, sanctions are lifted and measures to guarantee tourists' safety put in place, then the economically significant South Korean market may once again open.

In short, South-North Korean relations are now better than at any other time. Remembering how it was just a year ago, the present Korean Peninsula situation is astounding. Is peace coming to the Korean Peninsula? Yes, it is shimmering in front of us. Now the future relies on North Korea's active will, South Korea's cooperation and neighboring countries' support.

Once North Korea sincerely and specifically starts working on its denuclearization, international society, including the U.S., China, Japan, and Russia, will offer diplomatic security and economic assistance. Here, South Korea will continue its mediating role for the Korean Peninsula's peace and prosperity. However, this role requires economic symbiosis utilizing tourism and the manufacturing industry, security symbiosis by the declaration of the end of the Korean War and a peace treaty, and diplomatic symbiosis with North Korea and other related countries.

Published date: 2018. 08. 18

[INTERVIEW]

Russia still has role on Korean Peninsula issues

With Victoria V. Panova, Vice President, International Relations, Far Eastern Federal University (FEFU), Vladivostok.

By Jaeho Hwang

The Moon Jae-in government has three main foreign policies: the "New Economic Map", based on cooperation with North Korea; the "New Southern Policy", focusing on Southeast Asia and South Asia, and the "New Northern Policy", which concerns Russia and Central Asia.

In terms of promoting the "New Northern Policy" into serious progress, President Moon has established the Presidential Committee on Northern Economic Cooperation and attended the New Eastern Economic Forum conducted by Russian President Vladimir Putin in Vladivostok last September.

Next month, Moon is planning to meet Putin at the FIFA World Cup in Russia, where issues regarding North Korea and South Korean-Russian economic cooperation will be discussed. Here, Dr. Victoria V. Panova, Vice President for International Relations at the Far Eastern Federal University (FEFU) in Vladivostok, gives her view on Korean-Russian relations in this email interview.

Q. How do you evaluate South Korean-Russian relations since President Moon took over the presidency?

A. First of all, I need to mention that all the views expressed here are my personal views and are not expressed in my official position.

I believe relations between the two countries have all the conditions for deep, friendly and mutually beneficial cooperation. The initiative of nine bridges of President Moon could constitute a positive further development of such neighborly relations and more regular meetings of economic commissions, while Korean investor days held in the Far East are to serve the same purpose.

While South Korea occupies sixth place among Russia's trade partners, and over the time of President Moon in power total trade turnover between the countries continued growing at a much greater pace, a lot of that could be still attributed not just to the new policies implemented, but rather to a resurging Russian economy and higher prices for hydrocarbons.

It should be said that trade items composition remains unbalanced and more action should be undertaken by both sides in order to achieve even better results. According to Vice Premier Yu Trutnev, full potential of bilateral cooperation remains underexplored. Russia and South Korea also need to continue paying special attention to humanitarian and cultural exchanges and cooperation programs, enhancing people-to-people contacts, which in turn would foster further already very warm relations between the neighbors.

Q. What do you think of the recent inter-Korean summit?

A. It definitely was a very welcome move, and Russia and its people are very much interested in having peace and stability in the region, and this cannot be achieved without solving the inter-Korean problems.

But there are two things that make me cautious while evaluating its long-term effect. First of all, I remember previous similar meetings in 2000 and 2007 and the reverse of the process some time later. It is also worth remembering that a number of guarantees that the North Korean leader is willing to give cannot be obtained from his South Korean counterpart and need affirmative steps on the part of the USA.

At the same time there are at least two aspects that could contribute to sustainability of what's happened – cautious market reforms that President Kim Jong-un started introducing in his country at the start of his coming to power, and the logical end of the weapons' upgrade phase in North Korea, which would allow for tradeoffs within a comfortable zone.

Q. What do you expect from the U.S.-North Korean summit?

A. The expectations of the June 12th meeting of the two Presidents in Singapore were running high all the days between its announcement and its cancellation. Why would many people, even knowing the difficult history of the issue would still get into this euphoria and suggest that no matter how feeble and unprepared this summit looked, it would still bear real fruit?

Of course, it might have been the need to get positive news and hope for peace after the months of military alert and balancing on the brink of war with the exchange of harsh wordings and gestures of the previous months got everyone worried of the possible breakout. Thus, the total reverse of the course and agreement of the two leaders to meet and negotiate, all that after the hopeful Inter-Korean Summit, could have had additional psychological effect of something positive happening after risk of military outcome running high. A number of people would also say that state of reforms and general approach of the North Korean leader, aiming at taking his country out of isolation into the new brighter future also meant we are to have a successful summit.

What went wrong instead. Well, everyone even slightly not lazy would name among the reasons of the failure of holding the summit itself US-ROK military drills and Bolton's mentioning of the "Positive Lybian scenario". What is there to see, is whether we really had high chances for the Summit to work up to its expectations if it did happen.

Let's look at the President Trump. If it were for the regular country leader, I would say such announcements make us confident of the preliminary results already negotiated and degree of breakthrough leading to lasting peace and stability on the Korean peninsula being in final stages. At the same time, this is not a regular leader, but rather Donald Trump, known for his spontaneous activities. Which could on the one hand bring success to the meeting, but on the other hand there are a few "But" that should be taken into account. A) new set of people responsible for the region/ or issue area as a whole with just one month ahead for substantive preparations - we've just had recent incoming of the US State Secretary Mike Pompeo only few weeks back we've had Admiral Harry Harris appointed to become US Ambassador to South Korea; according to my knowledge we still don't have special envoy for North Korea after resignation of

Joseph Yun. B) Donald Trump is a hostage of his internal counter-revolution, which occurred when he came to power – any fault pas or even small mistake will be used by his opponents among American political elites to the full, and how much they will be willing to welcome the situation where North Korea makes partial concessions is to be seen

Nevertheless, what we see here, is that difficult issues, even if sometimes could be resolved due to unexpected and even illogical behavior of the leader, taking those steps, do plunge into even a bigger pit after early high hopes if failed. We should always remember – best improvisations are rehearsed ones. US – DPRK Summit and "Breakthrough" demonstrated this well.

Q. What's your anticipated outcome and agenda from the South Korea-Russia summit next month?

A. While it won't be anything but speculation, since it is not yet public, I'd see the upcoming meeting of the Russian and South Korean presidents as having a number of important issues on the table – including the situation around the Korean Peninsula, although more details will come up as the situation evolves. And as we saw recently, things change with cosmic speed. But also, there will be the first outcomes of efforts in deepening Russian-South Korean socio-economic and humanitarian relations.

Q. Where does Russia stand regarding the Korean Peninsula issue, including the peace treaty and the six-party talks?

A. Russia's stand remains unchanged, and it is about there being no other alternative to diplomatic efforts to resolve challenges surrounding the Korean Peninsula. The stance also includes full normalization of relations between the DPRK and South Korea, between the DPRK and the

USA, and also full adherence to six-party talks, since security in Asia concerns all players represented in this group.

Russia's role in the Korean Peninsula is small compared to other countries, but still it can never be ruled out. Currently, the Moon government plans to discuss the details of the Panmunjeom declaration with North Korea and the U.S., and the details of the peace treaty with North Korea, the U.S. and China. However, it is likely Russia will play a role in the establishment of a peace regime on the Korean Peninsula. In addition, the Moon government's main policy, the New Northern Policy, is aimed at cooperation with Eurasia but it is no exaggeration to call it the "Russia project". Russia is an important partner of the current South Korean government in terms of both security and economy. We can therefore expect a constructive role for Russia on the Korean Peninsula.

Published date: 2018. 05. 26

[INTERVIEW]

Pyongyang Declaration: Vietnam feels 'Misery Loves Company'

With Thanh Hai Tran, Senior Research Fellow, Diplomatic Academy of Vietnam.

By Jaeho Hwang

Vietnam, one of the major countries of ASEAN, is meaningful to Korea in several aspects. In economic terms, it is a significant investment region for Korea, and furthermore, as Moon's regime came up with the 'New Southern Policy', it now is important in diplomatic terms as well.

Close to China, Vietnam also shares the same strategic concerns with Korea as it stays between China and the United States. Vietnam has relations with North and South Korea and is in relatively positive shape with all. In addition, because it has gone through national division as Korea did, Vietnam might have observed the recent inter-Korean summit more than any other country.

The Diplomatic Academy of Vietnam is the diplomacy think tank, where we can find Vietnamese diplomatic policies and overall flows. Here, I interviewed Thanh Hai Tran, an expert on the Korean Peninsula; Deputy Director General, Institute of Foreign Policy and Strategic Studies; Diplomatic Academy of Vietnam.

Q. There was the inter-Korean summit this week. How do you evaluate this meeting?

A. The Third Inter-Korean Summit is a positive step toward building sustainable peace on the Korean Peninsula and strengthening mutual trust between the two Koreas. Chairman Kim Jong-un and President Moon Jae-in agreed to turn the Korean Peninsula into a "Land of peace without nuclear weapons and nuclear threats". The two countries vowed to "Cease all hostile acts against each other".

On the nuclear issue, Pyongyang pledged to destroy the Tongchang-ri missile engine test site and the Yongbyon nuclear site if the United States takes reciprocal measures. This again confirmed that North Korea continues to apply the "Salami slice" strategy and follow the principle of "Reciprocity". The ball is now in Washington's court.

We do not have either a timeline or any detailed guarantees yet. But I think the pledges Kim and Moon made at their third summit could inject fresh momentum into the stalled nuclear negotiations between Washington and Pyongyang and lay the groundwork for another meeting that Kim recently proposed to Trump.

Q. How do you anticipate the North Korea nuclear issue and the United States' North Korea regime guarantee?

A. The Singapore summit committed North Korea to giving up its nuclear weapons and the United States to guarantee North Korea's regime survival. However, this is not the first time both sides have made such a pledge. Washington and Pyongyang made the same commitments in 1994, 2005 and 2007. These commitments, nevertheless, were not realized, largely because of the difficulty in the implementation phase — what people call "The devil is in the details". The recent rapprochement between the United States and North Korea is encountering difficulties because North Korea is not willing to disclose its nuclear sites and the United States is pushing hard for denuclearization in the next few years.

The two sides have not yet agreed on the definition of denuclearization and guarantee. This means that there is a high chance the latest commitment will break down as in the past if the two sides fail to resolve their differences any time soon.

Q. One of the most significant features of Southeast Asia is the multilateral organization, ASEAN. Do you think a similar organization is possible in Northeast Asia?

A. ASEAN and its consensus-based mechanism reflect the characteristics of the Southeast Asian region which is comprised of small and medium countries. Unlike Southeast Asia, Northeast Asia is a region with many powers, a U.S.-led "Hub-and-spoke" security system and a security order largely based on the balance of power. The mistrust and strategic competition between the United States and China make it difficult to foresee a possible Northeast Asian version of ASEAN, at least in the near future. In short, an ASEAN version of Northeast Asia will only be viable if the security issues are resolved in a way that harmonizes the interests of major countries while paying sufficient attention to the interests of smaller countries.

Q. How do you see inter-Korean relations?

A. The recent improvement in inter-Korean relations is a major change and a welcome development on the Korean Peninsula. It helps reduce tensions and paves the way for the parties concerned to work towards a peaceful resolution for the Korean Peninsula. There remain uncertainties, and the two sides' commitment to improve bilateral relations does not necessarily mean that tensions will not recur. It is important that commitments be institutionalized through policy and action. Regional countries including Vietnam would be willing to assist the two Koreas in maintaining peace and security on the Korean Peninsula.

Q. What is the Vietnamese perspective/view of South Korea?

A. In the 1960s, South Korea was one of the world's poorest countries that heavily depended on foreign aid. However, over the past 50 years, South Korea has rapidly upgraded its industrial structure, transforming itself from a poor agricultural nation into a global leader in multiple advanced industries.

Today, South Korea is one of the G20 countries leading the global economy. This development success story has been underpinned by strong leadership and an appropriate economic development strategy. With complementary economic structures and many similarities in terms of culture and history, Vietnam and South Korea have enjoyed 25 years of diplomatic relations and nine years of strategic partnership. Although 25 years is not a long time in the history of the two nations, the cooperation between the two countries so far has strongly developed, especially in the economic field. With a solid strategic partnership founded on trust and mutual respect, the relationship between Vietnam and South Korea will

continue to build on past achievements and be further deepened in many areas, including trade, investment, culture, education and people-to-people exchanges.

Q. What are the issues in Korea-Vietnam relations? Do you have any suggestions for improvement?

A. As mentioned above, the relationship between Vietnam and South Korea is generally in good shape. However, there are two issues to which we need to pay attention. One is history and the other is trade relations.

First, the history issue between Vietnam and South Korea. As both countries have experienced war and a colonial past, Vietnamese and Koreans, more than anyone else, understand the sensitive nature of historical issues. Nobody wants this to become an obstacle to bilateral relations. Sincerity, mutual understanding and a future-oriented approach are the keys to overcoming historical issues.

Second is Vietnam's trade deficit with South Korea. Last year, Vietnam ran a trade deficit of about US$31.8 billion with South Korea, up 53.4 percent from the $US20.8 billion deficit of 2016. A trade deficit is inevitable because South Korea has emerged as the biggest investor in Vietnam over the past four years. However, an over-large trade deficit may have unhealthy implications.

One of the key solutions is to increase exports of Vietnamese products to South Korea. It is suggested that South Korean firms cooperate with the Vietnamese government to promote Vietnam's supporting industries, expand the network of local suppliers and help Vietnamese enterprises join global supply chains of South Korean conglomerates such as Samsung, LG and Hyundai.

Although the countries have signed a bilateral FTA, it is still difficult for Vietnam's export products to get access to the South Korean market due to technical barriers. Therefore, the South Korean government could consider lowering the technical barriers and help local distributors bring Vietnamese products to South Korean customers.

Through the interview, I could feel Vietnam's, and furthermore ASEAN's hope for North Korean denuclearization and a peace regime. Above all, this is because the Pyongyang Declaration between two Korean leaders was a step forward for peace in Asia. As well as the hope that Vietnam has, I could also see his concern that the way to peace will never be easy; because we all know that Vietnam has striven for independence and peace for decades and centuries.

The ways to unification differ depending on each country's respective historical conditions and domestic or foreign politics. However, Korea and Vietnam share sympathy for each other. Our expectation and wish for peace and prosperity is not just one country's obligation — it is the obligation of Northeast Asia and Southeast Asia.

The opinions expressed in this article are the author's own and do not reflect the view of the Diplomatic Academy of Vietnam or Ministry of Foreign Affairs of Vietnam.

Published date: 2018. 09. 22

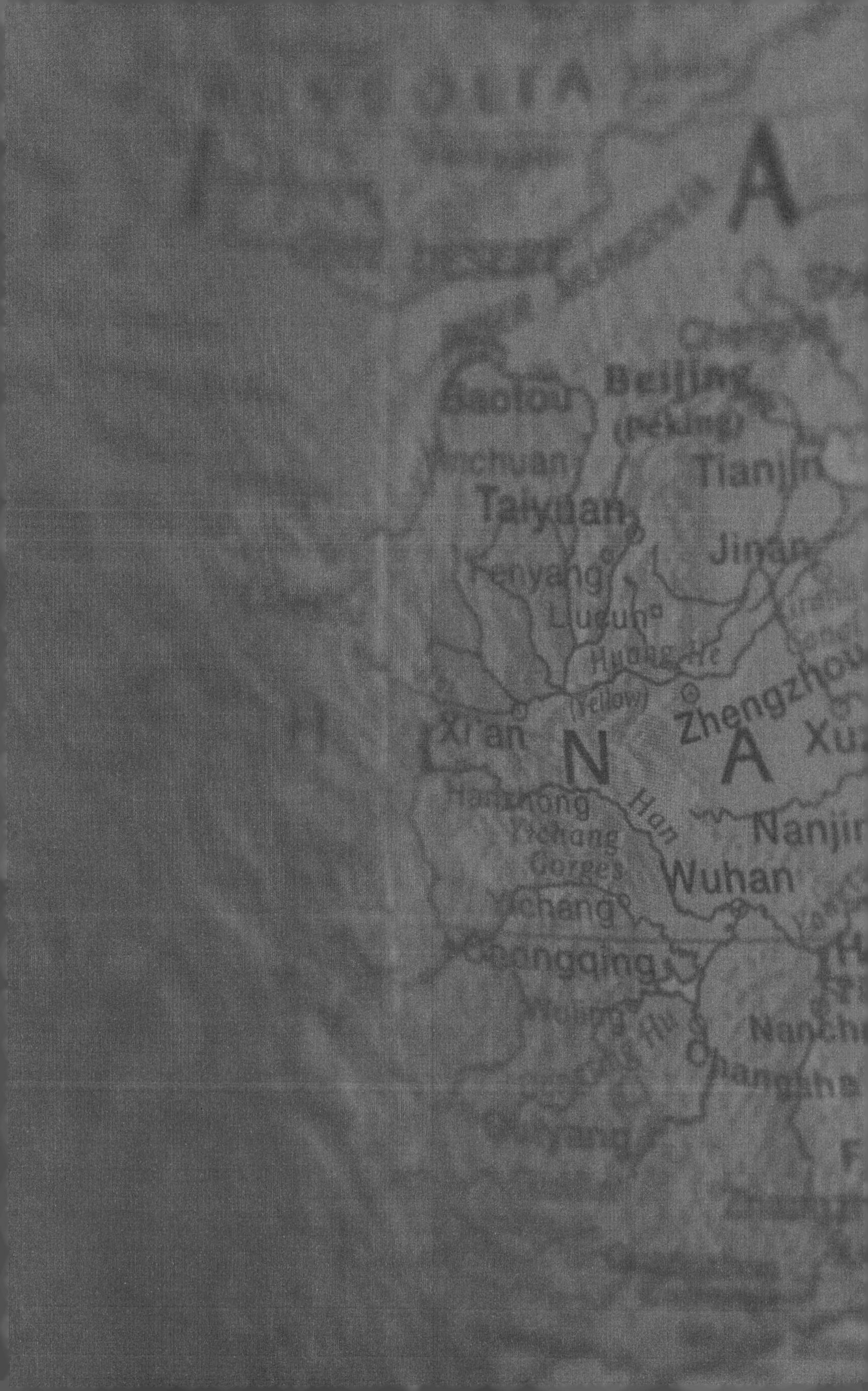
Beijing
(Peking)
Tianjin
Taiyuan
Jinan
Fenyang
Zhengzhou
Xi'an
Hanzhong
Han
Nanjin
Wuhan
Yichang

3

Public Diplomacy

China Watcher

3. 1. Universities

[INTERVIEW]

Globalization: Chinese universities develop strong policies

With Jiang Feng, Party Secretary,
Shanghai International Studies University.
By Jaeho Hwang

Korea currently hosts 100,000 students from around the world. Now the Korean government has announced its "Study Korea 2020 Project", to extend the numbers to 200,000. The government and universities are not alone in this effort. Neighboring China and Japan also pursue such policies.

The Chinese government is recruiting many students by providing scholarships. Both Korea and China are developing globalization policies aligned with their respective sizes, economic prowess, academic competitiveness, public diplomacy and educational policies.

In May, Jiang Feng, a longtime official at China's Ministry of Education, and party secretary of the Shanghai International Studies University (SISU), one of the major universities in China, sat with me to discuss the globalization of Korean and Chinese universities.

Q. Could you briefly explain the university education policy of China?

A. In recent years, China's higher education has experienced rapid development in quality and quantity. Statistical data shows that there were 2,631 regular higher education institutions (HEIs), including 470 private colleges, and 37.79 million students across China in 2017. The gross enrollment rate rose to 45.7 percent. Now the university education policy of China focuses on stabilizing the scale, adjusting the mix and promoting equality and quality. In 2017, China initiated the "Double world-class" (top domestically and internationally) project to elevate some universities and disciplines to a world-class level. Last year, the Ministry of Education of China issued several policies to build and improve the capacity of universities and strengthen the status of our four-year college education in the world. In addition, China is also investing heavily to revitalize higher education in less prosperous central and western provinces, supporting local universities and colleges to build their capacity to better serve local social and economic development.

Q. Is there an index to evaluate the globalization of Chinese universities?

A. Yes. The annual report of "University Rankings by Internationalization" (URI) is currently the most recognized ranking system, with a focus on university internationalization. Designed by the Evaluation Research Center for University Internationalization of Southwest Jiaotong University, the annual URI report has been published every year since 2013. In the most recent 2018 URI report, 139 Chinese universities are on the ranking list. URI ranks the universities internationalization according to seven key indicators: internationalization of students, faculty and staff, teaching, research, cultural exchange, international visibility and peer review. In this index, the numbers of students participating in in-bound and out-bound exchange programs, on-campus international students, faculty members with an overseas education background, joint research projects undertaken by university and international scholars, overseas campus and Confucius Institutions, annual budget on university international cooperation and exchange are all important criteria that are taken into consideration and analysis. We are encouraged to see progress on all indicators.

Q. How do Chinese universities manage international students and what is the composition of students from abroad?

A. Official statistics shows that in 2018 there were a total of 492,185 international students from 196 countries/areas pursuing their studies in 1,004 higher education institutions in China's 31 provinces/autonomous regions/provincial-level municipalities. Among these students, nearly 60 percent were from Asia, 16.57 percent from Africa, 14.96 percent from Europe and 7.26 percent from America. South Korea topped the list with 50,600 students, followed by Thailand, Pakistan, India, the United States, Russia and Indonesia. The number of international students in China who registered with degree programs has witnessed the fastest growth, accounting for 52.445 percent. In terms of major, Chinese language is the top choice for international students. But more and more international students study other disciplines, such as engineering, Western medicine, literature, economics, management, Traditional Chinese Medicine (TCM) and education.

Q. Could you compare the respective strengths of Korean and Chinese universities?

A. Universities in Korea and China have many things in common: we both face severe competition; we seek higher global rankings and good reputations — our international rankings have been rising on a fast track; we make great efforts to fulfill social responsibilities, and we have made ourselves increasingly indispensable in our nations' political, economic and social advancement. If I focus on Chinese universities, they are mostly public and receive regular funding from the central and the local governments. The number of students we recruit is predetermined and their quality is guaranteed and relatively consistent. Our faculty team is generally stable, with a low turnover rate. Korea has many more private universities than China, which means you have more freedom in the selection of students and are more ready to launch innovative initiatives in order to compete with other universities for students, faculty and funding. In recent years, both Korean and Chinese universities have been pushing forward in a drive to expand humanistic education and internationalization. I hope we can have more exchanges and dialogues to discuss, cooperate and learn from each other's endeavors.

Q. What is the vision of SISU for future development?

A. SISU aims to be a world-leading university with its special focus on global and area studies, delivering both impact and influence through international, innovative and interdisciplinary research and teaching. Upholding our mission to "Interpret the World, Translate the Future", we are committed to preparing future leaders and professionals with advanced language proficiency, extensive global knowledge, and deep intercultural understanding to shape international scholarship across the humanities and social sciences, and address critical challenges worldwide.

Q. Could you introduce SISU's history, its reputation in China and notable alumni?

A. SISU is known for being one of the earliest institutions where China's higher education in foreign languages took shape. Our pioneering history began in 1949, the year of the founding of the People's Republic of China, with the establishment of the Shanghai Russian School. Over the past 70 years, SISU has grown from that mono-disciplinary language institute into a national leading and globally recognized university in China for international studies. SISU's discipline of foreign languages and literatures ranks first in the subject evaluation by China's Ministry of Education. Our graduates, including a large number of high-profile diplomats, are at the forefront of China's international affairs, such as Mr. Yang Jiechi, former foreign minister of China, and Mr. Qiu Guohong, Chinese ambassador to South Korea.

Q. Please provide us with a brief introduction of yourself, including notable past and present positions and affiliations.

A. I was born in December 1962 in Shandong Province. I studied German at Shanghai International Studies University from 1980 to 1984. I received my PhD from Beijing Foreign Studies University (BFSU) in 2002. Prior to 2014, I was deputy director general of International Cooperation and Policy at the Ministry of Education of the PRC and minister-counselor at the embassy of the PRC in Berlin. Currently I'm party secretary of SISU, in other words, chairman of the University Council. In Chinese colleges and universities, presidents are responsible for the daily operation and function of all overall affairs with and under the leadership of the party committee. We also call this the university council. It is the role of the party secretary to chair the university council.

Published date: 2019. 07. 20

[INTERVIEW]

Yenching Academy, a flagship of Peking University's globalization

With Fan Shiming, Associate Dean, Yenching Academy, Peking University.

By Jaeho Hwang

China is rising. More international students are setting their sights on this old, yet modern, country and have decided to pursue their studies in China, where they can explore China's role in the world — past, present, and future. Amid this trend, Yenching Academy was established in 2014 and this year marks its five-year anniversary. On the beautiful campus of Peking University, Yenching Academy exemplifies the university's quest for excellence.

This week, I met Professor Fan Shiming, Associate Dean of Yenching Academy of Peking University.

Q. Could you briefly introduce Yenching Academy?

A. The Yenching Academy aims to build bridges between China and the rest of the world through an interdisciplinary master's program in China studies. This initiative brings together young people from around the globe who have demonstrated a talent for leadership and innovation. The academy's goal is to shape new generations of global citizens with a nuanced understanding of China.

The Yenching Academy provides full fellowships to its scholars and offers them a wide array of interdisciplinary courses on China. Working closely with their academic mentors, Yenching scholars create their own study paths by choosing courses from six research areas. Here at Yenching Academy, we are a residential program aiming to create a community for scholars to take full advantage of this unique opportunity by participating and engaging in campus life.

Q. As an international program, what are the targets for international diversity?

A. The Yenching Academy annually enrolls approximately 120 new scholars from both China and abroad. International scholars comprise roughly 80 percent of the student body, while scholars from China comprise the remaining 20 percent. The academy has already recruited four cohorts in total, with 440 scholars from 73 countries and regions and 222 universities.

Q. With such a diversified student body, language must play an integral part in the study process?

A. The academy offers an English-taught program. Meanwhile, Chinese language study is an important component of the Yenching learning experience. There is no Chinese proficiency requirement for incoming international students, however, Chinese language study is compulsory at the academy and international students will be placed into different levels of Chinese language courses according to their performance in the placement test at the beginning of the academic year.

Q. Besides diversity being a central characteristic of the program, what would you say are some other important characteristics?

A. I would say interdisciplinary learning and hands-on experiences are two important components. We aim to push China studies beyond the traditional boundaries defined by the humanities and social science disciplines.

On the one hand, we integrate resources from inside and outside the university. Within the program, scholars can choose disciplinary courses from different departments. To supplement these courses and broaden the horizon of our students, we invite professors from renowned universities and distinguished guests from all over the globe to deliver lectures and speeches to our scholars. On the other hand, students can participate in a variety of extracurricular activities and field studies, i.e. site visits to startup companies, career development guidance, interviews from various media outlets, all of which aim to facilitate personal and professional development.

Through a week-long field study trip to Xi'an, scholars gained a better understanding of the rich history and folk arts of the former dynastic capital. In Zhejiang, the scholars were impressed by the combination of oriental elements, traditional heritage of silk culture passed down by a new generation of Chinese entrepreneurs and China's fast-paced growth in international trade. After their trip to Sichuan, scholars gained a deeper understanding of the picturesque beauty of China's natural scenery.

All these trips help scholars gain exposure to different aspects of China. The field trips and research opportunities that Yenching provides for its scholars show that the classroom expands beyond that at PKU and can take place almost anywhere in China's culturally rich and diverse land. In essence, Yenching is not just a traditional master's program, we are pioneering the exploration of intercultural exchange.

Q. You mentioned earlier that the scholars choose courses from six research areas. What are those areas?

A. The six research areas are: economics and management; history and archaeology; philosophy and religion; politics and international relations; law and society, as well as literature and culture. Each Yenching scholar selects one of six research areas in the field of China studies and writes a thesis with guidance from a faculty adviser. A scholar's choice of research area does not affect course selection requirements, but will determine the type of master's diploma issued upon graduation.

Q. Could you elaborate more on the Yenching fellowship?

A. All admitted scholars receive the Yenching fellowship, which covers tuition, accommodation in the Yenching Academy housing, a travel stipend for one round-trip journey to and from Beijing, basic medical insurance, and a living stipend adequate to cover campus living costs and expenses related to field studies.

Q. What applicants are the academy looking for?

A. Successful candidates should have outstanding academic backgrounds and demonstrate strong motivation and potential to become leaders in their chosen fields. Candidates' personal statements should offer specific and persuasive explanations of how they could benefit from studying in our program. Evaluation criteria include academic merit, leadership potential, international experience and long-term aspirations.

Q. Is there any other comment you would like to add?

A. Yenching scholars are driven, passionate and innovative. There is a student-initiated flagship event called the Yenching Global Symposium. It's one of the world's most highly anticipated conferences, with applicants from more than 100 countries that consist of participants from other major fellowships and leading institutions.

Through courses at Yenching Academy, they gain a more holistic understanding of China and its unique stories, of which they can share in the future. These excellent graduates come to China with their own visions and hopes to better understand China; we cannot fail them. I feel obligated to shape them into global leaders with a nuanced understanding of China in the future. The question that is constantly on my mind is: What can the academy do to provide the necessary foundation into shaping them as future global leaders?

Published date: 2019. 03. 09

[VIEW]

Korean universities need to strengthen global competitiveness

By Jaeho Hwang, Professor, Hankuk University of Foreign Studies, Seoul.

The most important characteristic of Korea's higher education policy in the 2000s is internationalization. Korea wanted to work toward internationalization but also, internationalization was extremely necessary for the country.

The reason why Korea showed interest in internationalization in the area of education is due to the establishment of the World Trade Organization (WTO) and the spread of free trade agreements (FTA). The two trends allowed the country to open up its education sector to foreign players. Korea's international status and economic power were raised and universities started to show more interest in globalization and international competitiveness.

The Korean government's policy vision is to strengthen international competitiveness in higher education and cultivate global talent. In 2015, the Korean government announced plans to attract more international students through upgrading the Study Korea 2020 project. Korea plans to attract 200,000 international students by 2023 and create various internationalization models for domestic universities.

By strengthening the global competitiveness of Korean universities, Korea will be able to absorb the demand for Korean students to study abroad and provide opportunities for education in Korea. At the same time, Korea intends to revitalize domestic universities' entry into other countries.

The reason why Korea had no choice but to work toward internationalization is due to the sudden drop in the school-age population. In 2017, the birthrate hit 1.05, which is the lowest since 2005 when it was 1.08. Second, the university entrance rate, which is a representative indicator of the Korean people's will for education, is also rapidly falling. After peaking at 83.8 percent in 2008, it dropped below 70 percent in 2016, which has not happened for 18 years.

Last year, it was 68.9 percent. As of 2017, the universities' student enrolment capacity exceeded the number of high school graduates. Third, days when university diplomas guaranteed employment have ended. Since the financial crisis in 2008, the number of young unemployed increased and more people began to be skeptical about college education. Fourth, due to the decline in the school-age population, Korean universities needed to attract foreign students to overcome financial difficulties and increase the number of students.

Although higher education in Korea has grown overall, the level of internationalization and competitiveness of Korean universities is still insufficient compared with advanced countries. Currently, about 60 percent out of 100,000 Korean students are Chinese students, which shows how biased other countries are. The internationalization of Korean universities is mainly focused on memorandums of understating (MOUs) and there is no real exchange. They are focused on foreign exchange and attracting foreign students.

When looking at the actual curriculums and the programs, the proportion that foreign language courses and cooperation with foreign universities take are small. Internationalization of outbound forms such as internships and establishment of overseas branches of domestic universities are also insufficient. The absence of the government policy vision and passive internationalization of universities derived from the government's excessive control in this area are also problems.

Therefore, a new approach is needed by learning from past lessons. Here are some suggestions. First, the importance of local cities in this global era is growing. In addition to cooperation between central governments, sub-regional cooperation is also becoming more common. Local accessibility is easy and the connection between cities near the border area is becoming more critical. For example, sub-regional cooperation between Russia, Japan, China and South Korea can be established.

Customized education is needed. The international political environment is a hardware that is difficult to change. Also, most governments are under financial pressure and it is not easy for universities to receive special budget support from the government. However, it is not enough to complain and universities should work for best education even with minimum budgets. By considering the characteristics of different regions and cities, universities can carry out customized education through connecting with local governments and corporations.

Based on a specialized language education infrastructure, university education based on the characteristics of the region and the strengths of cities and universities should be provided. In this region, there are internationally important languages such Russian, Japanese, Korean and Chinese. The global language is English but second languages are absolutely important. Universities can train talented people by combining languages and majors.

In conclusion, universities must lead and deliver governments for successful implementation of national policies. There are many functions and roles of a university. It needs to be able to have a leading function by raising questions against and directing the society. It also needs to help with competition in the job market. In other words, it needs to catch several rabbits. To strengthen the global competitiveness of Korean universities, proactive proposals and practical actions of universities and scholars must be prepared.

Published date: 2018. 04. 21

3. 2. Culture and Events

[INTERVIEW]

Culture is the best answer for Korea-China relations

With Roh Jae-heon, Director, Korea-China Culture Center.

By Jaeho Hwang

It was 1992, during former South Korean President Roh Tae-woo's term of office, when Korea and China established diplomatic relations. This was one epoch-making achievement that brought both countries into a fate community in Northeast Asia; therefore, it is evaluated as the representative outcome of Roh's diplomacy toward North Korea. In 2012, Roh's son, lawyer Roh Jae-heon, established the Korea-China Culture Center and became director. Roh has contributed to strengthening bilateral friendship through cultural exchanges since then.

Q. The Korea-China Culture Center, what exactly is the mission?

A. It mainly focuses on cultural exchanges between Korea and China. Officially, it was founded in 2012 as a commemoration of the 20th anniversary of Korea-China diplomatic relations. Frankly speaking, till then I was only vaguely interested in China. I've studied and worked in the U.S., then went to Hong Kong. Hong Kong, of course, is quite influenced by China, but has its own strong color. However, as I took a part in the 20th anniversary ceremony, I could catch some sense that Korea and China have a shallow understanding toward each other. Both countries needed to build up some kind of a bridgehead or platform for further understanding, not only for my generation but also for the future generation. There have been a number of agent endeavors for Korea-China cooperation. However, the actual approach to culture was still running short. I personally thought that both of us shared a high level of favorable impressions; but the more I delved, the more I found there were many we actually weren't well aware of. That was the ultimate motivation for me to start the Korea-China Culture Center. Through maximizing the exchange programs, cooperation is expected to be enhanced more.

Q. Can you describe some works the Korea-China Culture Center has done so far?

A. One representative example is the entertainment program we had with China's CCTV around four years ago. China these days is not really a big fan of classical dramas, such as Peking Opera. As a result, CCTV created an entertainment program to promote people's interest. In the process of designing the program, a Korean entertainment production company jumped in. After categorizing Chinese classic drama into three (Peking Opera, Yueju Opera and Sichuanese Opera), six Korean and four Chinese celebrities were grouped as a team. Their goal was to learn and produce a successful performance at the end. I consider this exemplar very refreshing and future-orienting, because it exactly points the direction for the fusion of different cultures. The new upcoming generation of the Korean wave should reflect "Universal value", which can embrace every difference, not only those which are 100 percent "Ours". In this sense, this program was a worthy start.

Q. I guess there must have been some difficulties for the Korea-China Culture Center during the THAAD issue?

A. Well, actually, it wasn't only our problem. The overall society had a hard time, but what really matters is always the feelings and sincerity. The policies can be deregulated and amended, but already changed minds and attitudes are terribly hard to re-attract. At first, I didn't consider THAAD (a U.S. missile defense system installed on South Korean soil) would have such a serious effect, because it was a matter of security and arms. Nevertheless, the harsh emotions surrounding this issue were heading way deeper and deeper; for both countries, I mean. As we could often see from the media, I also think both of us have responsibility on this. Since the matter could not stay in the original political arena, where it in fact belongs, the hard feelings spread over to other sectors as well. In the past, China had great feelings toward Korea, but what you see these days is most of them turned quite negative. I understand the feelings cannot always stay favorable. Though President Xi Jinping referred to Korea as “Korea, like a close relative’s home”, we still can sometimes have confrontations. In other words, I’m saying we might have possibilities of second and third THAAD issues. When we have misunderstandings and look at the problems emotionally, the answer cannot be clear. All sectors, including government, media and others, have to come together for better solutions.

Q. Can you share some of the current events you are planning?

A. In August 2016, we opened the Silk Road Chinese Movie Theater and play three to five Chinese movies every month. We try to reflect the period and audiences’ responses, so our monthly movie curation is based on different genres, directors, actors and so on. With the accumulated Korea-China movie industry’s related human resources and infrastructure, we opened the 2017 and 2018 Korea-China Scenario Forum during the Busan International Film Festival. As 2017 was a chilly year due to THAAD, we could hardly invite Chinese movie-related participants and start a Korea-China exchange. Now we will continue developing what we do and make more informative content for a stronger bridge connecting the two countries.

Q. What is the biggest difference between Korea-China culture?

A. The young generation in China is amazingly impressive. The reason I consider they are progressive is that they are fluent and honest in what they think and speak, no matter the age and status of the other. They are open to creative action and comments or demands without being conscious of their positions. When I think of the Korean young generation, it would be better if their circumstances could evolve like the young Chinese; because, from time to time, the juniors cannot even speak during meetings. I once thought Chinese young people must be less expressive or less creative because of the communist system, but I was totally wrong. Now I think maybe we are the ones who are drawing limits to ourselves.

Q. We started diplomatic relations with China in August 1992, when your father was the Korean president. This event is still evaluated as an incredible point that changed Northeast Asian regional order.

A. The beginning of Korea-China diplomatic relations is more significant in the sense that we came to provide new circumstances in the relations with North Korea rather than Korea-China's bilateral aspect. It is more like an establishment of diplomatic ties within a macro perspective. Looking over Korea-China's bilateral relations, during the last 26 years we had several cases that both countries are responsible for; which we couldn't have even imagined in the last 5000-year long history. Korea received enormous benefits thanks to China and vice versa. Both Korea and China have contributed on dynamics to each other in the flow of history. However, now is a momentous period; everything will proceed differently from the past. When we think of relations with China, we must overcome the limits of security or economy and head for strategic decisions for the sake of both nations and their peoples. Then the question is, how to approach China. the answer is through delicate and specialized steps.

Q. Is there any other comment you'd like to add?

A. There are plenty of experts who are very familiar with Chinese issues. Since China has a huge territory, enormous population and many fields of endeavor, the experts from various areas distribute the works. That's how we can guarantee sustainability. Furthermore, we must cooperate. Although we divide our fields, we have to gather up and march along together. We should do what we are best at, and walk together.

Director Roh is a very appealing figure to China. Under President Roh Tae-woo, 1992 saw the climax of Korea's policy toward the North. Korea started diplomatic relations first with the Soviet Union, then Eastern Europe and ultimately accomplished them with China. China then was isolated from the international community due to the Tiananmen Square incident in 1989. It was desperate for technological aid after opening up and reforming and diplomatic relations with Korea provided a window of opportunity. President Roh greatly contributed to Korea-China relations; now his son is aiming to play a role in the area of culture. I look forward to him being an exemplary and symbolic player in Korea-China relations.

Published date: 2019. 01. 26

[INTERVIEW]

The Korean Cultural Center in Beijing at forefront of soft-power diplomacy

With Han Jae-hyeok, Director, The Korean Cultural Center, Beijing.

By Jaeho Hwang

As we move through the 21st century, within each country's foreign policy, the use of soft power in public diplomacy and cultural diplomacy has been held in great regard.

The "Power to reign in people's hearts", also known as "Soft power", is the ability to shape the preferences of others without force or coercion. It is especially effective during exchange and cooperation between our nation and other countries with different cultures and systems. It also holds great significance for us when dealing with China, not only geographically our immediate neighbor but also an important influence on our economy and issues of reunification.

The Korean Cultural Center, Beijing, is where cultural diplomacy and, possibly, public diplomacy is put into practice directly in China. The director of this center is Han Jae-heuk. He also is minister counselor of the Korean Embassy in Beijing. He was former director-general for public information policy, Ministry of Culture, Sports and Tourism, and consul at the Korean Consulate in Hong Kong and Shanghai.

Q. What do you do at the Korean Cultural Center, Beijing?

A. At the Korean Cultural Center, Beijing, our main job is to introduce Korean culture in China and promote cultural exchange between Korea and China. Immediately after Korea and China established diplomatic relations in 1993, the Korean Cultural Center, formerly known as the Korean Culture and Information Center, was founded on a smaller scale in a leased office floor in Beijing. Today, we are based in a freestanding office building with four stories and two underground levels, equipped with the most modern facilities and equipment in downtown Beijing. We run a variety of exhibitions, performance events and all kinds of class programs to introduce Korean culture.

Q. Could you describe the programs more specifically?

A. At the Sejong Institute, there are 20 classes that teach beginner and intermediate-level Korean language courses. We also offer 10 free Korean culture courses in Korean traditional dance, taekwondo, gayageum, Korean calligraphy, etc., to teach the local people about Korean culture. For popular classes such as cooking classes, online registration fills up in a matter of minutes. As we enter the third semester for this year, over 1,000 Chinese individuals have registered for classes, and for the past 10 years over 20,000 people have registered. As the center attracts international visitors, the open-minded middle class and younger generations who work in the city, we operate a wide range of programs to meet the needs of the mainstream.

During lunch break time, we offer Korean classes, culture classes and courses dedicated to K-pop and hallyu-style makeup. Along with hosting movie screenings every weekend, we invited famous directors and actors for post-screening discussions. Every month, through weekly Korean culture-related events, we've hosted traditional performances, indie bands and musical performances, classic performances and poetry readings. Moving away from offline promotions, every day we share news to our 30,000 members on Chinese multi-purpose messaging app Weixin and WeChat about exhibitions hosted at the culture center, along with news on Korean culture, arts and tourism.

Q. Marking the 26th anniversary of diplomatic relations between Korea and China, how is the current state of affairs between Korea and China in cultural, sports and tourism exchange?

A. In a few weeks, August 24 will mark the 26th anniversary of diplomatic relations between Korea and China. For the past 26 years, diplomatic relations between Korea and China have rapidly advanced with an unprecedented growth in diplomatic history. What served as the leading role was the cultural exchange between the two countries and its people. In the past, the people did not understand each other very well, but now, if you were to converse with most Chinese people living in cities, they are familiar with Korean cuisine such as kimchi, bibimbap and bulgogi, and would have heard of places such as Seoul and Jeju and dramas like "Jewels in the Palace".

Among the younger generation, we have met people who know more than us about K-pop, K-dramas and K-movies. Recently, even in Korea, in addition to learning about traditional Chinese culture, Chinese pop culture has drawn attention, with channels dedicated to Chinese dramas available to the public. Although two years ago relations between Korea and China faced difficulties and affected exchanges in the culture and tourism sector, we have seen gradual recovery after President Moon Jae-in's state visit to China last year. During the visit, the two heads of state enjoyed cultural performances from a world-class orchestra and artists from Korea and China, and experienced the harmony of Korea-China cultural exchange.

Q. Could you introduce your most recently held event?

A. To mark the upcoming 26th anniversary, our biggest event was held this year in early July, with the Korean Embassy in China and the Gansu Provincial Government jointly hosting a large-scale Friendship Fair event. With an opportunity to host an event in Lanzhou, the culture center held a variety of performances in taekwondo, traditional dance, beatboxing and b-boying with up to 50 performers, and the center received great praise from the 4,000 locals who attended the event. By hosting a lecture with South Korean Ambassador Noh Young-min at Lanzhou University, and setting up tourism exhibitions of our highest-quality agricultural and marine products, cosmetics and hallyu-related products at the local trade show, our events kept pace with the China Western Development and Silk Road Development. Prior to this event, the local government and organizations in Harbin also held Korea-China culture exchange seminars and cultural arts performances.

Q. What was the most rewarding experience of your career?

A. Immediately after formally establishing diplomatic relations in 1992, it was the first time a South Korean president made an official

Beijing-sponsored state visit to China. During this time, I remember the bright eyes of Chinese university students showing great interest in learning about Korea, and I also remember when I was first dispatched to work at the culture center and can visualize the faces of young students and the elderly participating in our newly opened Korean language courses.

Though nowadays people in China are much more familiar with Korean movies, dramas and K-pop, dramas such as "What is Love" was broadcast nationwide on the CCTV network from 1997, and K-pop concerts, such as H.O.T performances, had only been picked up in the late 1990s.

What's fun is that in some ways being the director of the culture center is being a salesman of our culture. Yet it is good to see the sales involve the depth and significance of our culture. From traditional music and dance to modern films, dramas, webtoons and cultural industries, to even Korean food and fashion, recognition of our artists in a variety of fields in culture, art and sports on a global scale has made me so proud. Nowadays, we often meet the Chinese arts community while visiting local Korean restaurants, or at the center, eating and having traditional Korean tea and meals, taking the example of our own customs of sharing delicious food with our neighbors. When we meet, I introduce the high culture of Korea to China and am often told how happy and fun it is to enjoy time together.

Q. What do you most want to accomplish during your term in office?

A. We intend to develop more integrated cultural events. At the end of last year, we held a city documentary screening and photo exhibitions, in addition to poetry recitals and folk song concerts featuring Jeju haenyeo (women divers). We received feedback that the attendees were deeply impressed with the various forms of culture that depicted the lives of haenyeo and the natural human environment of Jeju.

At our folk painting exhibition, attendees learned how to draw, with folk art painters creating an interactive cultural experience. We want to use these types of participatory and integrated methods to expand our exhibitions and performance events. We also wish to expand on interactive cultural exchanges. For performance events, rather than using a one-sided approach in showcasing just our culture, we always include Chinese culture in the programs so that everyone can enjoy each other's culture. It is important to share and understand one another through this interactive approach.

To conclude, "Soft-power diplomacy" is one country's diplomacy directed toward the people of other countries in contrast to traditional diplomacy, where one country's diplomacy is directed at the governments of other countries. If successfully pulled off, it is extremely urgent to secure the friendly sentiments of the people of other countries. These past few years, both Korea and China have had reservations due to the THAAD deployment issues. Soft-power diplomacy alone is not enough to quickly resolve doubts about each other and restore sincere relations. At the forefront of soft-power diplomacy, we look forward to the power and effect of the more active public and cultural diplomacy of the Korean Cultural Center.

Published date: 2018. 08. 04

[INTERVIEW]

Beijing People's Art Theatre: Where cultural public diplomacy holds

With Liu Zhichen, External Affairs Manager, Beijing People's Art Theatre.

By Jaeho Hwang

On March 5, we happened to discover that a grand book fair was going to be held in the Beijing People's Art Theatre to celebrate Prime Minister Zhou Enlai's 120th birthday.

Since my research area is China's diplomacy, I had a personal interest in Zhou Enlai, the godfather of China's diplomacy. He was the reason I took the train all the way from Beijing to Tianjin, a while after China and Korea established diplomatic relations in the 1990s, to visit the "Memorial to Zhou Enlai and Deng Yingchao".

The title of the introduced book in the recent book fair was "Zhou Enlai and Beijing People's Art Theatre". I didn't attend the book fair, but could remember the Beijing People's Art Theatre. Then, fortunately, I came to meet Liu Zhichen in Seoul, who is in charge of external affairs at the theatre. Here is an interview with her.

Q. I heard you are in the theatrical industry in Beijing. Would you please introduce yourself and the specifics you work on?

A. I'm Liu Zhichen from Beijing. After graduating from the Beijing International Studies University in 2010, I got a job at the Beijing People's Art Theatre. Here, my main position was in the show planning team, especially dealing with international exchange performances. For the last seven years, I have projected the showcases of the Beijing People's Art Theatre's international festivals, which are the very superior products in this capital theatre. For example, there were Russia's Moscow Art Theatre, St. Petersburg Alexander Theatre, Israel's Gesher Theatre and Belarus' Janka Kupala National Theatre who came to Beijing to perform. The tasks I deal with the most are connecting and arranging the meetings with the respective countries' consuls in China. During the talks, we build up the contracts by selecting the performance teams and organizing other extra works. In addition, I support the technical aids, discuss marketing tactics and host the visiting teams once they arrive.

Q. People consider the Beijing People's Art Theatre as the Seoul Art Center in a Chinese version.

A. As a national theatre company of China, Beijing People's Art Theatre owns its unique performing style. The theatre was established on June 12, 1952, and the famous dramatist Cao Yu was its first president. Ever since its establishment, the theatre has put on nearly 300 ancient and modern plays of different styles, which are from both home and abroad. From the 1950s to the 1960s, the theatre was famous for putting on works by Guo Moruo, Lao She and Cao Yu. The representative productions include "Tiger Tally", "The Teahouse", "Peking Man", "The Death of a Popular Beijing Opera Singer" and Western plays like "The Miser", "Aesop", "People with Gun", "Even a Wise Man Stumbles", etc.

Since the 1980s, a group of excellent artists of the young generation has emerged. During this time plays including "Weddings and Funerals", "Uncle Doggie's Nirvana", "The Top Restaurant", "Birds Men", and others went on. The theatre also introduced Western plays including "Amadeus", "Death of a Salesman", "The Gin Game", and "The Caine Mutiny Court-Martial", etc. Among these, many have been performed over 100 times, and were given awards like the national "Wen Hua Award", "Five-one Best Works Award", as well as the "Gold Chrysanthemum Award" and the "Literature and Art Works Award", given by the Beijing municipal government.

The theatre company now has three theatres mainly for drama performances: the Capital Theatre, the Mini Theatre and the Experimental Theatre. The theatre's stage art center has a professional production base, which can make sets, costumes and props for the theatre itself and also for other performing troupes.

Q. How is the international troupe exchange environment?

A. The "Beijing People's Art Theatre International Festival" is the brand program managed by the performance centre of the Beijing People's Art Theatre since 2011. Each year it invites both foreign and domestic theatre companies and groups to perform their classic plays, which not only offers an opportunity for Chinese theatre practitioners to learn from each other, but also shows the Chinese audience excellent plays from all over the world. With eight years of effort, this brand program has been highly recognized by both industry and the audiences and it has become a high-

light of Chinese drama industry. The festival has already invited troupes from Russia, Israel, France, Britain, Belarus, Poland, Romania, Lithuania, Serbia and so on. Therefore, the theatre has established a cooperative relationship with artists and organizations all over the world and gained recognition. The Capital Theatre has already become the first choice for many world first-class theatres as their performing place in China.

Q. What are the Beijing theatre's criteria on collaboration with foreign plays?

A. Recently, we went to the "Edinburgh International Festival" in the U.K., the "Avignon Festival" in France, the "Radio Romania International's Festival", and another arts festival in Israel sequentially. During this tour, we extended out partnership to France, Russia, Poland, Lithuania and Slovenia. Our prior show selection principles were mostly oriented to 'the well-known play, theater and director', but the latest choices are more with the literary values. The worldwide popular plays such as "Tempest", "Don Juan" and "The Lady of the Camellias" were all performed in the Beijing People's Art Theatre. Not only these, but other literary works with ethnicities had favorable responses from public in our theatre. For instance, playwright Mickiewicz, who is famous as a Polish poet in the 19th century, wrote the epic "Dziady", which mirrored the folk ancestral rites customs of old Poland. The play written based on this epic is "Suitcase Packers", which Israel's Camel Theater performed at our place in March 2013. The stage settings and general management were following the old-fashioned Polish culture, which does not exactly fit into the public's taste these days. This play is quite difficult for modern society to understand that only a few audiences could bear till the end. Maybe a very dark stage where you can barely see the show was one reason people left. Nevertheless, we knew it was worthy enough to deserve a show in our theatre because this play has an unimaginable influence in Polish history.

Q. Can you give some evaluations on Korean theater?

A. The most impressive point of the Korean theatrical industry is the perfect market operation. From marketing and advertising, to selling tickets, the systems are just excellent. For instance, the promotion team kept handing out flyers not only on the streets but also inside the theaters. Talking about the advertisements, the theatre-related posters and other materials were everywhere, from the streets and subways to extra public places. The performance information is easily accessible on the internet and the ticketing process is very well described that the customers could purchase with no difficulties. Secondly, the standards of stage acting and the techniques are very sophisticated. The movements were delicate, the skills were talented, and I could see how various dance and techniques were applied for one performance. Then, that the play was taking a pretty large part of Korean public culture was impressive. As many Koreans were interested, so many people paid a fortune for plays even on the weekdays though the price was not so cheap. Also it had a very mature public culture. There's one example I remember. When I went to the musical "Gwanghwamun Sonata", the age spectrum of the audience was all the way from young to old. This actually means a lot, because it means it can bring sympathy from all different generations. In short, this proved the shows are deeply sitting inside Korean audiences' hearts.

Q. Any other comment you want to share?

A. Both Korean and Chinese play-related institutions must have learned and applied Western theories and knowledge; however, they clearly are distinguishable. In the future, I see the necessity of two countries' performance exchanges among staff or universities, so they can watch and explore each other's market operations, performing systems, or expression on the stage. So far, a considerable number of play-related students are registering for exchange programs, which is a smart idea. In this sense, I personally wish Korea and China can share the vision of this art industry by interchanging and developing what each has accumulated.

In conclusion, China as a socialist state, throughout the interview, I could see it was not only influenced by the Soviet Union's politics and economics but its culture as well. Since 1978, after reform and opening, Chinese society went through massive interactions with Western countries that changed Chinese culture in diverse aspects. Especially during Xi Jinping's era, the government fully supported plays so that the field expanded its international connections and could adopt developed countries' fine technologies. This can be interpreted as China's enthusiasm to make qualitative improvement beyond quantitative growth.

From the Korean play market's perspective, expending its international volume through China as well as contributing to Korean play development into the Chinese market might be an unexpected opportunity for Korea's cultural and public diplomacy, along with economic outcomes.

Published date: 2018. 07. 01

[REVIEW]

China's 'Reform and Opening Up Exhibition' leaves lasting impression

By Lee Dong-gyu, Research Fellow,
Institute for Global Strategy and Cooperation.

"The International Exhibition of China's Reform and Opening Up in 40 Years", co-hosted by the China State Council Information Office and the Chinese Embassy in the Republic of Korea, was held at the National Assembly Members' Office Building from January 31 to February 2.

About 130 vivid pictures of China's reform and opening up were displayed under three themes — history, development and cooperation — graphically presenting the country's historical route and various achievements from 1978 to 2018.

The opening ceremony, which started with the welcoming message by Qiu Guohong, Chinese Ambassador to the Republic of Korea, brought about 200 people together — politicians, government officials, experts and students from the ROK and China.

Ambassador Qiu introduced the developmental progress and remarkable achievements of China's reform and opening up and stressed that China would continue to implement these through cooperating with other countries. Particularly, he said that the two countries should intensify strategic communication and invigorate mutual cooperation in each field, citing the proverb, "After the storm comes the calm".

In his congratulatory message, lawmaker Sul Hoon (Democratic Party of Korea) noted that 40 years of China's reform and opening up have led to a dramatic change in human history and he hoped Korea and China would prosper together like the past 5,000 years.

Public Diplomacy Ambassador Bahk Sahng-hoon also delivered a congratulatory message. He said Korea and China have something in common — astonishing economic growth. As Korea performed the Miracle of the Han River, China achieved the Miracle of Reform and Opening Up during the past four decades. He closed his message by expecting the two countries' close cooperation for peace and prosperity in Northeast Asia.

China is the world's second-largest economy and accounts for 15 percent of total global GDP. Nobody can dispute the fact that China is serving as a center for world economic development. China's economic rise is based on its consistent reform and opening up policy. Various pictures of reform and opening up in the exhibition provided visitors with a rare glimpse of how the policy has created

China's unprecedented development and improved its people's quality of life.

Exhibition visitors first experienced the historical route that China has taken during 40 years of reform and opening up. This is shown through diverse images of China's change from the beginning of the policy to now, such as the Shenzhen Economic Zone in 1979, the Pudong District of Shanghai in 1992 and the Shanghai Free Trade Zone in 2013. The most impressive photo was about Dongdaqiao in Beijing, which demonstrated the past and the present by mixing a black and white picture of the Dongdaqiao department store, built in 1981, and a color picture of a shopping mall built in the same location in 2016.

The exhibition also helped visitors sympathize with the Chinese people's emotions of happiness and hope. Despite of its rapid economic growth, most people in rural areas still are struggling to meet their basic needs.

The photo of President Xi Jinping, who discussed measures to eradicate poverty in November 2013, proved that China is a developing country as ever. Nonetheless, the Chinese people's delightful smiles in the exhibited pictures seemed to demonstrate what they feel about their future is not despair or lethargy but hope and expectation. Of course, there are many remarkable achievements of reform and opening up, especially in economic and technological fields. The most marvelous achievement, however, may be to restore the Chinese people's pride and expectations for a bright future.

Lastly, the exhibition stressed win-win cooperation between China and other countries. With its economic growth, China continues to maintain a more than 30 percent contribution to global economic growth. Photos of China's economic cooperation and cultural exchange showed that reform and opening up not only are beneficial for China itself, but also have provided other countries with opportunities to obtain economic profits in the era of economic interdependence.

The exhibition was held on a smaller scale than I expected. But it successfully showed that the path of reform and opening up that China has maintained since 1978 is the right one for the country by focusing on developments and achievements in the past 40 years and it reconfirmed China's will to continue implementing the policy.

What will China be like after another 40 years of reform and opening up? I expect it will continue walking the path of further reform and opening up to achieve win-win cooperation with its neighbors and global society, as shown in the exhibition.

Published date: 2019. 02. 16

3. 3. Locals and Enterprises

[INTERVIEW]

The butterfly effect of Chinese social enterprise for regional peace

With Kim Hor Toh, Chief Architect, Temasek Holdings.

By Jaeho Hwang

The enterprises, which run its business with the social vision to develop the regional quality of life, are referred as the social enterprise. There are not a few big and small social enterprises throughout the West as well as in Korea. However, China is just at its inchoate level for this type of business.

Considering China's socialism, which puts a priority on the social contribution rather than blindly seeking profit, this seems quite plausible. Since 2000, many Chinese companies have begun pursuing social responsibility, and here I introduce who has had this spirit from the beginning.

Kim Hor Toh was born in Malaysia, studied in the U.K., Singapore, and the U.S., and now usually works in Hong Kong and in mainland China. He is an architect and urban planner working in China's real estate sector. His passion for sustainability led him to start up a social enterprise to promote Sustainable Development Goals 11 in China. Kim's research interest also covers the intersection between security and development. He believes that only by establishing a firm foundation for peace, can societies flourish and developments be sustainable in the long term.

Q. Please tell us about your background and work experience.

A. I am an architect and urban planner by profession and have experienced the rapid urbanization of China over the past 20 years. The World Bank estimates that over the next two decades, its urban population is expected to increase by 250 million. How will China deal with such rapid urbanization from the viewpoint of Sustainable Development Goals 11?

Q. Your resume gives the impression of a keen interest in peace and social values. First, with regard to your interest in social values, what is the guiding principle of the Center for Environment and Development Studies?

A. The center was set up as a response to under-served needs by small and medium sized cities in China to access world-class consultancy services for the built environment. It is still in a startup stage. We undertake our mission based on the guiding principle of "Humanitarian competition", which was elucidated by the educator Tsunesaburo Makiguchi. As a concept, it confronts the reality of competition, which socialism has inadequately taken into account as a source of energy and vitality. Social enterprises, which are aligned with the principles of humanitarian competition, harness competition while ensuring it is conducted firmly on the basis of social values, thus bringing forth a synergistic reaction between humanitarian concerns and competitive energies.

Q. Although there is an understanding of the term "Social enterprise",

can it also be considered an emerging trend in China? What is the operating environment like for social enterprises within China?

A. Li Fan, adviser to the Leping Social Entrepreneur Foundation and co-founder of the Global Links Initiative, the first social entrepreneur membership organization in China, believes that social enterprises will become an emerging trend as China continues to reform its market-based economy. The social enterprise sector in China is still in its infancy but I believe the government recognizes the value of social innovation to co-create solutions to the many social challenges confronting China. So, I am hopeful that the regulations governing social enterprises in China can be developed further, especially for international social enterprises.

Q. What are some rewarding experiences you have had while running a social enterprise in China?

A. It is always very rewarding when you see your efforts create a social impact in society. In my case, getting the local government bureaus in the built environment sector to agree with the ideas I have proposed to create more sustainable urban environments is indeed fulfilling.

Q. Second, a question relating to your interest and contributions to peace. I was introduced to you by IISS when you attended the Shangri-La Dialogue in Singapore last year. I am quite curious why an architect and urban planner like you has a keen interest in security issues?

A. My research interest is also focused on the intersection between development and security. In a report released at the International Conference on Climate Security in the Asia Pacific region held at Seoul in 2013, at least 110 countries considered the effects of climate change a "Serious national security issue". Natural disasters as well as man-made disasters such as armed conflicts can severely impact developments. Therefore, I believe that only by establishing a firm foundation for the peace and security of the land, can societies flourish and developments be sustainable in the long term.

Q. You attended the Shangri-La Dialogue again this year and then Singapore hosted the DPRK-US Summit a month later. Recently President Moon Jae-In delivered a lecture at ISEAS in Singapore. What is your impression on President Moon's initiatives for peace and the denuclearization of the Korean Peninsula?

A. I admire President Moon-Jae-In's master class diplomacy in making peace and denuclearization of the Korean Peninsula based on the Berlin Doctrine a reality despite the many challenges ahead. I hope the international community will also support President Moon's peace efforts and the denuclearization of the Peninsula. For example, in a peace proposal authored by peace builder Daisaku Ikeda, he called for all countries in the Six-Party Talks to declare Northeast Asia a nuclear non-use region as a step toward denuclearization of this region, which includes the Korean Peninsula. I hope China, the only nuclear weapon state with a no-first-use policy, will boldly initiate this to create physical and psychological security, not just in the DPRK but also for those countries relying on the nuclear umbrella.

Q. Would you like to share any additional comments or insights?

A. About achieving the Sustainable Development Goals (SDGs) in this region, Daisaku Ikeda in his peace proposals also concretely called on South Korea, China and Japan to join together to create a regional model that will embody best practices that can be shared with the world.

At present, there are 151 local government sister-city agreements between South Korea and China. For South Korea, China and Japan combined, there are now more than 600 sister-city agreements. I look forward to see more cooperation among the Northeast Asian countries to achieve the SDGs.

Chinese social enterprise has just taken its first step forward, and the path and direction for its development is still being debated. For further growth, massive theoretical studies in academia and experience in the field are required. So far, many experts in the field have been unable to come up with certain agreements; it is meaningful that the social enterprise, as a non-profit sector, uses market operation measures in order to coordinate the resources, manage the market mechanism, and to realize the public vision. Considering the reality where the market economy promises to compensate individuals' effort while materialism also dominates, this humanism-based challenge, which tries to combine the national interest with profit, would certainly be worthy.

The attempts and outcomes will one day bring the butterfly effect within society, within a nation, and stretch to the region. It will eventually bring co-operative development and stable peace among the nations in the region.

Published date: 2018. 08. 11

[INTERVIEW]

Future of Sino-Korean Relations, Exchange of Local Government

With Park Byung-eun, Head, Beijing Office, Governors Association of Korea.
By Jaeho Hwang

Korea and China are geographically and culturally similar, but as they have different historical experiences in the process of industrialization and modernization, there are quite a number of differences between each other. Nevertheless, for the peace and prosperity of the entire Northeast Asia as a neighboring country, both must establish a solid cooperative relationship. In order to achieve genuine mutual understanding and cooperation, I believe that the most important thing is to build a bridge of understanding and consideration between the peoples of the two countries. There are several exchanges at the central government level, however, it is now difficult to regard China as just a 'whole' because China is extremely large with massive population. As the importance of private and public diplomacy is growing, exchanges between the two countries' local governments are gradually expanding and becoming more significant.

In response, Park Byung-eun, a councilor at the Embassy of ROK in China, as well as the head of Chinese office of the 'Governors Association of Korea', examined the current status and possibility of local exchanges between South Korea and China.

Q. What exactly does the association work on?

A. The Governors Association of Korea was established on January 23, 1999 as a consultative body consisting of heads of 17 metropolitan and provincial governments nationwide. It aims to contribute to balanced development of local communities and sound development of local autonomy by promoting exchanges and cooperation between cities and provinces and supporting joint consultation and internationalization of local governments. In particular, as in exchange and cooperation with China, we are holding annual Korea-China Local Government Exchange Conference, Korea-China-Japan Local Government Exchange Conference, and Korea Heart to Heart (K2H) Korea local government training projects. The Korea-China Local Government Exchange Conference is greeting 16th anniversary this year, starting since 2002, and the Korea-China-Japan Local Government Exchange Conference is a meaningful meeting that has history and tradition since 1999, so meets the 21anniversary already. In addition, we have held the Korea-China Governor Conference since 2016 every other year to maintain a strong friendship between the leaders of the two local governments.

Q. How far is the history of Korea-China Local Government Exchange Conference?

A. The Korea-China Local Government Exchange Conference has been held annually since 2002. It is hosted by the Governors Association of Korea, the Embassy of ROK in China, Chines local governments, and the Chinese Foreign Ministry. The first meeting was held in May 2002 in the Guangxi Zhuangzhu autonomous district with 24 participants (9 Koreans/15Chinese). From 2003 to this year, the conference was held in several other regions, and this year it is held in Guizhou Province in August with 227 people (82 Korean/145 Chinese) participated.

Q. What were the past achievements and difficulties of the Korea-China local exchange?

A. Since Korea-China diplomatic relations were signed in 1992, the number of friendships and sisterhood between the local governments has reached 645 cases, which is 39 percent of the total friendship agreements the Korean local governments have with around the world. In addition, more than 90% of the Korean local governments have engaged in exchange projects in various fields with Chinese local governments by signing friendship or sisterhood exchanges. The exchange between local governments has been carried out in various areas, considering the characteristics of the region, including administrative, youth, cultural, and market reforms. The greatest achievement of the exchanges between Korea and China is that they have deepened the understanding of each other and promoted development through mutual solidarity and cooperation. It is true that local government exchanges have the advantage of unshakable continuity, even if there are conflicts between the central governments. However, in the event of conflict between the two countries, such as THAAD, the exchanges were also definitely affected.

Q. What is the difference between Korea and China in terms of local governments?

A. There are two main differences. The first is that in the case of Korean local governments, each local autonomous government can pursue international exchanges independently, while in the case of China, the autonomy or independence of local governments is a bit lower than ours. For example, if an international conference such as the Korea-China Local Government Exchange Conference is held, it must be approved by the Chinese Foreign Ministry, and if the local government of China desire a sister city with a foreign local government, it must also obtain approval from the central government and higher-level local governments in advance.

The second is continuity of international exchange work. In the case of the Chinese local government, the government employees in charge of international exchanges are responsible for the work continuously in order to enhance the professionalism. In other words, if there are no special circumstances, the staff of the foreign affairs will work in the foreign affairs for the rest of their lives. However, since Korean local government is operating under a rotational position system, the length of time that our local government employees are in charge of international exchange work lasts for only two years.

Q. Would you recall a memorable episode?

A. Various exchange projects are being carried out between two countries' local governments. Among the all, the most memorable business is human exchange. Under the auspices of the association, we have been promoting the Korea Heart to Heart (K2H) program since 1997, which is to invite local government officials from overseas and train them for six months in Korea. From 1997 to 2019, 866 people from 30 countries participated, and 583 of them were from Chinese local governments. In June 2017, we held the "K2H Human Resources Forum" to celebrate the 20th anniversary of the K2H program. At that time, a Chinese local government official who participated in the first K2H program in 1997 presented his experiences with the K2H program, as well as how it has influenced his current working career. His remark was not just a shared experience of Korea-China exchanges, but a vivid record of how the exchange actually grew and developed.

Q. Is there any particular direction or business the association is aiming for?

A. The project that I would like to focus more on in the future is to promote local people's awareness of the need for international exchange by dealing the realistic and current issues. For example, the growing problem of international marine waste along Korean west coast is an issue that both Korean and Chinese local governments are facing jointly. In order to solve these problems, we are required to build network of heads of local governments on the west coast, so that they can act in a practical way and create a forum for relevant discussions and implementation.

Published date: 2018. 10. 26

3. 4. Language and Communication

[INTERVIEW]

Life of Korean-Chinese interpreters and the future of interpretation

With Kim Jin-ah, Professor, Korean-Chinese Translation, Hankuk University of Foreign Studies.

By Jaeho Hwang

As a frequent participant in international conferences, I am well aware that the success of a meeting is in excellent presentation. However, I also know that interpretation is no less important than the presentation itself. The atmosphere of the meeting becomes absurd if the interpretation is awkward, although the presentation is excellent. Especially, unless the interpreter is familiar with the terms that are highly specialized, such as the military field, not the general subject, the entire meeting faces a challenge. On the other hand, the conferences excel if the delicate nuances of words and sentences can be well delivered. Moreover, when Chinese idioms are rife among national leaders and national interests are sharply at stake, if the sincerity is reflected and intention are conveyed, the translator deserves the highest sense of worth and pride.

I met Kim Jin-ah, professor of Korean-Chinese Translation at the Graduate School of Translation at Hankuk University of Foreign Studies, who has considerable experience in the field of interpreters among national leaders and in the field of educating the interpreters. She was recently selected as the first Korean expert in Tianjin City's Chen Yin planning, receiving support from the Chinese government for three years and contributing to the development of Chinese translation studies. We talked about the lives of interpreters.

Q. Would you explain the meaning of simultaneous interpretation in academic and professional value?

A. Simultaneous interpretation is when an interpreter in the booth listens to the speaker outside the booth from the receiver, and at the same time uses the microphone to deliver the message with correct interpretation. Simultaneous interpretation requires an extremely high level of expertise, and in this sense, we can name it "A comprehensive art of communication". Being fluent in both languages doesn't mean you can translate at the same time, but you need to be highly trained for your instant reaction, concentration, logic, memory, and expressiveness. In addition, simultaneous interpretation requires timeliness, and within a given time, the content must be expressed in very fluent terms. Therefore, more than the basic qualities that simultaneous interpreters must have, they must be capable to cover the knowledge of the various fields, be professional in mind control and psychological warfare, which are not swayed by any tense situation.

Q. What is the future for simultaneous interpretation? Is it possible that technological advances such as AI threaten the market?

A. In the era of the 4th Revolution, the simultaneous interpretation market has also entered the era of customized technology from mass production, and we are now being challenged to be superior to AI. Previously, simultaneous interpreters had crossed the boundaries of all fields rather than their own specialty. However, now we are in need of the interpreters who have their own expertise area and can make accurate and sophisticated translations to suit the customer's level and needs. As AI technology advances, the simultaneous interpretation market is expected to change greatly as well. If we use the strength of AI to seek cooperation rather than considering it as a threat, we can look forward to achieving synergy and another leap for the market. For example, translation can be assisted by systems in Google or Never. However, on the other hand, we can think of raising post-editors or result evaluators who can revise, correct, and evaluate the results. Then hopefully there should be an effort to transform them into operators who run the AI.

Q. How do you anticipate the market for Korean-Chinese simultaneous interpretation? How do you draw the prospects?

A. It has been 40 years since Hankuk University of Foreign Studies established the Translation Graduate School, in 1979, a training institute for simultaneous interpretation of international conferences. The Graduate School of Translation at Hankuk University of Foreign Studies is a private school, but it has fully served as a state institution to train translations, such as Tongmun-gwan, which was established during King Chungryeol's reign in the Goryeo Dynasty, and Sayeok-won during the Joseon Dynasty. Many national level professional interpreters who were educated for the last 40 years are working in the simultaneous interpretation market in Korea. However, as the number of professional resources is growing, the competition in the domestic translation market is expected to intensify. To survive within this competitive landscape, the further translation market will have to look for the following. 1) We need to move beyond the domestic market and step into the overseas markets. Indeed, translation companies are also making inroads abroad as Korea's leading companies, Samsung, LG, and SK are entering the foreign markets. A broader overseas expansion and the preparation and effort should be made accordingly. 2) Industries that are becoming new growth engines in Korea are drawing attention and are expected to open and expand the translation market. For example, it is expected that there will be advancement for professional interpreters to fields such as medical translations, legal translations, and refugee translations. 3) Another new translation job can be considered, such as the post-editor, who cooperate with AI for better results. While demand will expand in all other industries, including games, finance, legal, and software, it is expected that the order of interpreters will be established as demand for more specialized and competent translators increases.

Q. I heard that the simultaneous interpretation market is growing in China. Can you explain this sensation going on in China?

A. In 1992, when Korea and China established diplomatic ties, only a few Korean language departments were established in China, but now more than 280 universities have Korean language departments. As China changes from the world's factories to the market, the translation market is expanding as well. As major international conferences are being held in China's big cities, interpreting has been acknowledged as a highly paid and coveted job. To catch up with the trend of the market quickly, many universities are promoting the establishment of a Master of Translation (MTI). China strives to learn and train from the countries that are advanced in the field of translation, and work on cooperation to develop this area. To develop an industry in a single field, China has been creating a sensation throughout the country by running regular translation training programs for Korean language professors, brisk academic competitions, and inviting experts.

Q. May I ask when you personally felt proud of being an interpreter? Do you have any particular anecdote to share after the establishment of diplomatic relations or during the Korea-China Summit?

A. There are numerous episodes, ranging from the 1983 emergency landing of the Chinese plane in the ideological era, to a meeting in 1992 with Chinese Premier Wen Jiabao and business leaders, or the simultaneous interpretation for the 17th and 18th Presidents' inauguration ceremonies. But above all, I am still appalled with the mistake I made during a live broadcast in 1992, when Korea and China were establishing diplomatic relations. I was listening to the situation of satellite broadcasting on KBS and simultaneously interpreting to the entire nation, so the mistake should not have been made. I think rather than the achievements, the biggest mistake I've ever made is left as a more unforgettable episode.

Q. Do you have any other comments?

A. Although the perception of interpreters has improved, some users still do not recognize the characteristics of translation and are not very considerate for the translators. The speakers are obliged generously to supply the materials to interpreters beforehand, and because their words are conveyed through translators, it is absolutely necessary to consider interpreters by trying to slow down the speed of speech and stop at where it is appropriate. Nevertheless, sometimes different data or material are presented without any notice. For instance, the previously given data is A; however, B is presented at the last moment. Furthermore, whenever a theory, plot, literary expression, or proverbs are quoted in the content, the translator confronts difficulty in expression if not informed in advance. I wish the users would keep in mind that cooperation is the only way to complete the mission.

Published date: 2019. 10. 12

[REVIEW]

Chinese feel Korean-Chinese friendship through Korea poems

By Ko Sung-hwah, Researcher,
Institute for Global Strategy and Cooperation.

In the summer of 2018, Korean Culture Center in Beijing hosted the first "Feeling Korea, through Poem" Contest. This contest was opened to members of the public who are interested in poetry, and to other professional poets and writers. As the title indicates, the purpose was to make a big step forward in Korean-Chinese literature exchange and cooperation. The Korean Culture Center in Beijing held the awards ceremony last September.

Fortunately, a small booklet of 29 outstanding awarded collections came into my hands. More than 1,000 poems were submitted from all over China, written by people of many ages: from very young primary schoolchildren to seniors. Most offered a colorful presentation of Korea in various topics and areas.

This first collection consisted of four main parts. Part 1: Telling the Poem delivered congratulatory messages and evaluating comments. The contributors were deeply moved by how Korean-Chinese friendship can be blended through the melody of poetry, and expressed a wish that the afterglow of these poems would flow peacefully and widely. In Part 2: See through the Poem, Chinese experts contributed their pieces of art; showing Korean nature and charm or the grandness of Korean history. Part 3: Feel with Poem was where the awarded poems were presented. They covered the diversity of Korean culture and local beauty. Part 4: Photo Story introduced photo collections that represented Korean colors and features that harmonized with the poems.

Among the professionals' works, I'd like to present a short work from Sun Xiaoya's "Smile of Bodhi".

"We just gazed at one another in silence.
We laughed heartily gazing each other.
Our laughter planted silent barley (bodhi)".

It is always amazingly attractive how Chinese-Korean translation can sometimes bring different meanings that all make sense in the context. It seemed like the poet was presenting this poem to a particular friend; nonetheless, in terms of Korean-Chinese relations, I found it somewhat impressive. Although it was short, it was strong.

In the non-expert section, Yang Wan-ning won the Special Award for Korea-China Exchanges with "The Legend of Hallasan".

It admired the mystique and sanctity of Hallasan and its warm and motherly embracement, then beautifully connected the previous life to the present through the term legend.

Luo Zichen won the golden prize, on one hand delicately drawing the stature of the Silla Statue of Buddha under the moonlight and sunset; on the other, describing with wild tones the turbulent history that the statue has gone through. The harmonized balance of differentiated color was expressed with vividness.

Silver prizes were given to The "Flavor of Haeundae", "Hahoe-tal: River, Flow Freely", and "Yeongbokgung at Sunset".

Bronze prizes went to "Bring back Gangwon-do", "Seoraksan", "Imgangseon· Feeling Korea through Poem", and "Time in Seoul".

There were 10 other excellence awards that included prose poems.

Going through the poems, I again realized how close Korea and China are in sentiment. The burning passion from "Jeju Seongsan Ilchulbong Tuff Cone", the clear and cool air from soft winds at "Naksan-sa Temple", and the stillness of cloud and moon could be naturally imagined from their words.

In addition, the writers had a high understanding of Korean

history and historical relics. Quite a few pieces covered the agony of Korean history. It is always interesting how different people, especially those from different circumstances, can share the sympathy.

Another thing that caught my attention that the term "Friend" appeared frequently. As the value of friendship counts in Chinese culture, the poems also represented its worth.

As Lee Yuseung, professor of Beijing International Studies University, wrote in her evaluation, both Korea and China have a long history of appreciation of poetry. She added, "We are here, continuing the long tradition of composing a poem in East Asian culture. And now we are standing in the flow of the appreciation".

South Korea has been a friend of China for a long time. We sometimes had difficult times but we have stood in the flow of history together. To be a closer friend than ever, understanding each other's deeper thoughts and reading the minds comes first. In this context, cultural exchange is where friendship can be sustained with the lowest risk, especially when we see the language. This "Feeling Korea, through Poem" must build closer emotions and sympathy.

An extract from a poem by Pu Sang, an expert poet, will close this review.

What is a poem?
Poem is a lonely adventure in your mind.
What is a poem?

Poem is a secret hallway the poet found.
You might meet someone there at times.

"A Fate, laid in a Poem"

Published date: 2019. 03. 16

3. 5. Multi-Cultural Society

[INTERVIEW]

Multi-cultural families: a potential strength for Korean society

With Choi Young-nam, Principal,
Daedong Elementary School.

By Jaeho Hwang

One out of 14 Koreans is in an international marriage — more than 7 percent. This is numerical evidence that Korean society is becoming more accepting of international marriages compared with the past.

Nowadays, we see celebrities who are married to non-Koreans, and fluent Korean-speaking foreigners through TV programs. Along with the media, many organizations have campaigns that might steadily change our perspective on multicultural families.

In the past, we were used to distinguishing "The foreigners" through their skin color and thought they could not get along with Korean society. However, the bias and repulsion have certainly vanished in some areas.

There is a special elementary school in Seoul that has a majority of children who come from multicultural families. It is Daedong Elementary School, established in the 1980s. Daedong is in Yeongdeungpo and is designated a "World Citizens School" by the Seoul Education Office. Its reputation is famous among multicultural families. This week, I met the principal of Daedong, Choi Young-nam.

Q. Would you briefly introduce today's Daedong?

A. The number of Chinese students at Daedong has dramatically increased compared with four to five years ago. Back in 2015, the ratio of multicultural children (who come from international marriages or foreign parents) was less than half. However, today we are recording 318 out of 445, which is about 71.5 percent. Among the 318, 95 percent of parents have Chinese nationality. We have 302 (67.9 percent) Chinese, 127 (28.5 percent) Koreans and 16 (3.6 percent) who come from other countries, including Southeast Asia. So the rumor that every Daedong student is Chinese is totally untrue.

Q. How are you operating Daedong? Is there any particular way?

A. I was appointed as the principal of Daedong on March 1 this year. I still remember that day. It was a pretty heavy burden for me to work in Daedong back then, because of Daedong's unique conditions. However, as I live my everyday with them I see Daedong children's manners and purity as a considerable merit. Also, how parents respect teachers actually comforts the mood in Daedong. Though the academic achievement might be slow, teachers and administration members feel very stable with the parents. Now my vision is to strengthen the weak. While thousands of Koreans are heading to China to learn Chinese, why don't we develop our special conditions to improve ourselves? My ultimate goal is to build Daedong into a place where children with various nationalities can light-heartedly come and learn.

Q. Are there any difficulties caused due to cultural differences?

A. I don't witness particular cultural collisions, but know there is big difficulty in the language barrier. In this sense, many of the students are in fact falling behind in the standard academic levels, in such as Korean or math. To overcome this inevitable barrier, we are having afterschool supplementary classes and operating a program at library where senior students can voluntarily read the books out loud to the juniors. This actually works very well and builds bonds among students. Besides the academic part, we are also having a "Let's Commend" program for healthy minded growing. In this little box of compliments, anyone from friends and teachers to parents can freely participate. We systemized this program that every week we select the most highly laudable student and officially share compliments through the school broadcast. Similarly, we united our greetings to each other as "Love you". By doing so, we are encouraging and letting them know they deserve respect and being cared for.

Q. What is the main obstacle Daedong is facing?

A. The toughest difficulty is definitely the negative views on multicultural families and Daedong from society. Especially, since the parents usually maintain their Chinese nationality and get job visas, most people consider they only exploit benefits such as free meals and free compulsory education until they go back to their country. In addition, the majority of the Korean parents whose children attend Daedong do not have positive thoughts on the image Daedong has: the "Multicultural School". Since Yeongdeungpo is one of the deteriorating areas in Seoul, lack of budget and human resources, and serious deterioration of facilities are urgent matters which must be solved soon.

Q. What might be most necessary for Daedong's development?

A. Of course budget. I recently submitted the application for support to the city council. Because we need a globalized faculty, we are in need of more support in that. Furthermore, liberalizing the curriculum will help Daedong to operate smoothly. Though all the Korean elementary schools share the same subjects in the same frames, a blanket application to Daedong is quite harsh; it might be more efficient if we could liberalize a little.

Q. Is there any other comment you'd like to add?

A. I personally consider myself as a pioneer of a multiculturalized Korea. In other words, I feel fruitful but on the other hand have some kind of obligation to navigate Daedong in the right direction as a role model. There still is a lot to do. Many programs must be systemized to be settled. Then my dream is to lead Daedong into being a public globalized elementary school. In our efforts, we are trying to improve public awareness by planning a sustainable campaign that will see Daedong recognized as a school where children wish to come.

Korean people are generally referred as the "One" ethnic group; but now it would not be easy to say that. Korea has maintained its people, language and cultural community based on similar values and view of the world. Nevertheless, since the 1980s, thousands of foreign laborers rushed into the country and young foreign women also came in. Today, there are more than 2 million foreigners in Korea, which is 4.2 percent of the total population.

At the same time, the social adjustment of the increasing number of multicultural children is a key point for Korea's further development. If Korean society can successively integrate them, they will provide potential energy for future development. If it fails, it will create the social conflict that many Western countries are now grappling with. In this globalized world, a multicultural society might be competitive since it is based on diversity. If we strengthen these factors, it will be to our advantage. I support Daedong Elementary School's brave efforts to achieve success.

Published date: 2018. 11. 18

[INTERVIEW]

A Korean Chinese couple's Korean dream has come true

With Jin Songgen and Jin Zhegshu, Restaurant Owners, Dongdaemun, Seoul.
By Jaeho Hwang

The night in Dongdaemun station is no different from any other region in Seoul. The neon signs around the station are blazing, but the only difference is that the signs are in Chinese.

Most of these signs are for restaurants, especially Huo Guo, which means shabu-shabu. I've enjoyed visiting Huo Guo for quite a long time and have known the owners for almost 10 years. They are husband Jin Song Gen and wife Jin Zheng Shu. I always shared greetings with them and ordered a full table of food, but never had an opportunity to hear of their personal life; how they came to Korea, why they settled in Dongdaemun, or how they lived with their two children.

Ethnic Koreans living in China (Josunjok) settled in the three northeast provinces of China to escape the Japanese colony's military pressure in the late 19th century. They continued their lives after 1945, the year of Korea's independence, and started returning to their motherland when the ROK and China established diplomatic relations in 1992.

However, due to being away from Korea for a long time, the frustration they felt in Korea in gaps of culture, generation and wealth was beyond what we could imagine. During the challenges they went through in this country, many may have buckled to the invisible discriminations, but there also were quite a few success stories. Here, I interview this Josun-jok couple who accomplished their dream in the Huo Guo restaurant.

Q. What was your main trigger to come to Korea?

A (Husband). After being discharged from military duty, I had been doing several jobs in Longjing, but then longed to have a higher quality of life. Therefore, in 1999, I decided to come to Korea through paying 70,000 yuan to a broker. That is almost 14 million won in Korea, which is big money. Usually, these brokers swindle the desperate people, but I was the lucky one.

A (Wife). I came to Korea around the year 2000 from Tumen because I wanted a better life as well. In my case, my mom already had Korean nationality, which let me get Korean nationality relatively easier than others.

Q. How did you settle down in Korea and what were the obstacles you had to face?

A (Husband). When I entered Korea, getting a stable job was not easy. As a result, I used to work as a day laborer, such as a carpenter or in the construction field. Even after I met my wife that was my usual life. After all, in 2008, we opened this restaurant, which was about 10 years after we came to Korea, and then we married in 2010.

A (Wife). When we talk about Koreans' bias against Josunjok, it is beyond our thoughts. Regardless of how old you are, as soon as they find out that you have our accent, Koreans' way of speaking changes immediately. I used to work at restaurants as a server and could personally feel discrimination; for example, when the ingredients do not seem fresh enough, they asked me if they came from China. I've spent all my money to come to this country and the only thing I had was my ego. However, sometimes when people gave me sympathetic looks, I instinctually showed somehow an aggressive attitude. I remember one time that people asked me whether I knew what a banana was. (laugh) My answer was, "In China, even pigs do not eat them". Can you imagine how hurt I was when I was answering that negatively? It took exactly 10 years for me to overcome the complex of this bias.

Q. Is there any tips for your success? What is your ultimate goal?

A (Husband). It was never an easy success. For the first 10 years, we worked without any time off, or dared to spend money. We went through failures several times, especially when we challenged for developing this restaurant into a brand approximately seven years ago; it was one great adversity. Back then, we could not fully reflect Korea's regional sentiments or characteristics. We have changed our strategy into expanding only the few selected chain stores by distributing the recipes and ingredients with a low price.

A (Wife). We still struggle with the consulting or advertisements, but above all, "Coexistence" is our major motto and that's how we currently have 10 chain stores. We know that "We can survive when they survive", therefore, we provide good quality with a lower price. When we build the contract with the chains, we see how trustful the person is. Besides the trust, another main success factor I am proud of is our own sauce recipe, but I cannot share this with anyone (laugh). The flavor is not exactly the same as in China because seasonings come from Korea, but we stick to its original taste by hiring people from the mainland. Also, one other factor is globalization. Back in 2008, there was one Korean coming out of 10 Chinese. However, nowadays it goes the opposite way because people became more familiar with Chinese food and the world is getting smaller and smaller. If our business continues in good shape like this, my ultimate dream is to possess our own house, not rent. Then my children will be able to live in more stabilized conditions, not like us.

Q. How is the current Josunjok community in Korea?

A (Wife). Until the late '90s, there were not many ethnic Koreans living in China. Other than the first compatriot, most of them in Korea were illegally staying. As the number of migrants increased steadily, it largely grew during President Roh Moo-hyun's open policies and loosened regulations. Originally, there were about 2 million of us in Yanbian, but now there are less than 1 million in Yanbian and more than 1 million in Seoul. Nonetheless, the thing is that only a few of them were able to stably settle down in Korea. Most of them are in construction fields, just like my husband was at first. Exceptionally, there are quite a number of settlers in Garibong-dong and Daerim-dong who are in the restaurant business as we are; this is why we decided to settle down in Dongdaemun-gu.

Q. Is there any particular difference you see between Korean and Chinese education for your children?

A (Wife). Our kids are 10 years old and the other is five. I always teach them that "People come prior to the study". They learn Korean but will not start learning Chinese until they can perfectly master Korean. However, because I wish them to go to university in Korea, I let them learn English: the must-learn language. I am well aware of China's fame regarding the Tiger Mom, but personally consider Koreans are way worse. In China, the public schools give a bunch of homework so that kids do not have enough free time, while Korean kids also do not have free time because they are all sent to the private schools. In addition, the college attendance rate in Korea is extremely high that when they grow up, they only look for a better job though there is plenty of work you can do physically. Even in my restaurant, when we recruit employees, only foreigners come to apply.

Q. Do you have any other comments?

A (Wife). Korea is transparent, respectful and liberal. This is what makes Korea a very attractive country. However, Korea is soft with law execution; it really needs to be strengthened. Seeing Korean movies dealing with second convictions, it makes me concerned about our future society in which my children will live in. Personally, I expect to see that money never allows acquittal.

A (Husband). I just wish that Korea-China relations develop and stay positive. Considering how difficult it was to invite cooks from China during the THAAD period, macro-diplomatic relations always hit the petit bourgeois, just like us, who are at the very front line.

This couple now runs 10 chain stores. Though they stumbled on their way to success, they built up their maturity and skills in business. On one hand, they never let go the Korean traits of tenacity for success, investment for their children and gifted diligence. On the other, they knew how to build up the network among people through trust and expand it to their business, which is guanxi (network), the distinguishable culture the Chinese have. They were very well aware of the way to maximize both countries' advantages. I look forward to seeing their dreams turn into a small, but positive impact on Korea-China relations.

Published date: 2018. 10. 06

Beijing
(Peking)
Tianjin
Taiyuan
Fenyang
Jinan
Zhengzhou
Xi'an
N
A
Han
Wuhan
Yichang
Chongqing

4

Conclusion: Korea's Diplomacy Forward

C h i n a W a t c h e r

4 Conclusion: Korea's Diplomacy Forward

[INTERVIEW]

Korean diplomacy: Looking ahead

With Yoon Soon-gu, ROK Deputy Foreign Minister.

By Jaeho Hwang

It has always been a rocky road toward peace and prosperity on the Korean Peninsula, and so far it seems this year is no exception. Following the no-deal summit in Hanoi, the U.S. Treasury Department appeared to add new sanctions relating to North Korea, to which the North responded by abruptly withdrawing its entire staff from an inter-Korean liaison office. It seems now that the two countries are carefully weighing their options, studying each side's every move.

Deputy Foreign Minister Yoon Soon-gu sat with Professor Jaeho Hwang of Hankuk University of Foreign Studies, Korea Times columnist, last Thursday to assess the present state of Korean diplomacy and discuss the way ahead. Apart from having served in some key government posts, such as ROK Ambassador to Egypt, Consul General in Washington, D.C., and Director-General of the International Policy Bureau of the Ministry of National Defense, Yoon also holds a master's degree in international affairs from the Pennsylvania State University.

Q. Starting with the Hanoi Summit, what is your assessment?

A. I want to look on the bright side first. I believe it definitely provided an opportunity for the two leaders to better understand what is at stake for each side. This is crucial in setting up a solid foundation upon which future negotiations can take on further steps. The Korean government seeks to continue its efforts toward achieving complete denuclearization and establishing a permanent peace regime on the Korean Peninsula, with the help of the international community.

In this regard, let me remind you of the 2017 U.S.-DPRK Joint Statement signed in Singapore — at least three terms laid out in this latest statement are seeing sound progress. First, the ongoing recovery of the remains of U.S. soldiers; second, progress on U.S.-DPRK relations; third, narrowing the gap on the prospects for a lasting peace regime on the Korean Peninsula. In regards to denuclearization, the two sides are also putting up efforts to make common ground. I anticipate much better outcomes to follow.

Q. Lately, the term "Facilitator" is often being used to describe South Korea's role in U.S.-DPRK relations.

A. There have been various terms describing South Korea's role in regards to U.S.-DPRK relations. One of them, for example, was "Intermediary", but some may say it seems rather odd for a U.S. ally to be "Mediating" the two countries' relations in the middle. We also must not forget that South Korea is perhaps the biggest stakeholder in U.S.-DPRK relations. It is in our every interest to exert our utmost efforts to make things better between those two countries. Taking into consideration all these factors, the term "Facilitator" seems like the right fit.

Q. Recently, there has been discord between South Korea and China over the fine dust problem. How would you assess Korea's current relations with China?

A. I would assess that our relations with China have dramatically improved since President Moon's visit to China in 2017. For one thing, the sheer number of Chinese tourists, which had once been reduced over the THAAD controversy, is now on a recovery path. China is a crucial partner in our efforts toward achieving denuclearization on the Korean Peninsula, and the ROK government is in great appreciation of China's constructive role in this regard. As to the issue of fine dust, it would be most ideal for the two countries to discuss various joint actions that could be taken, such as joint research on possible solutions. This year, in recognition of the 100th anniversary since the establishment of the Shanghai Provisional Government, we seek to further expand opportunities for our mutual cooperation with China.

Q. Things have been pretty tense between South Korea and Japan lately.

A. From a long-term standpoint, there have been ups and downs in ROK-Japan relations. There is no denying, however, that Japan is our very important neighbor and that maintaining good bilateral relations will be beneficial to both sides. For this reason, the Korean government is taking a two-track approach by distancing history issues from our two countries' substantial relations with each other. Let me point out there were approximately 7.5 million Koreans that visited Japan solely last year. Even in times of hardship, I am generally optimistic that things will get better, considering the consistent level of people-to-people and cultural exchange between the two neighboring countries. Building on this, trilateral cooperation among Korea, China and Japan will also be instrumental in Korean diplomacy.

Q. China's "Belt and Road Initiatives (BRI)" and the U.S.'s "Indo-Pacific Strategy" seem to be holding each other in check. What should South Korea do?

A. Keeping in mind that we, as a nation, are hugely dependent on the geopolitical environment surrounding us, it is in South Korea's diplomatic, economic and national security interest to maintain a stable international system in Northeast Asia. South Korea is a small-scale liberal economy whose security and economic interests are closely interlinked with those of the international community. Any external impact on the current international system based on multilateralism and free trade will directly influence our national interest. That said, the Korean government is open to various possibilities and options that cross paths with our "New Southern Policy" and our openness to multilateral cooperation. The determining factors will be whether such options meet our national interest and whether they converge with our fundamental values, such as openness, transparency, diversity and norms-based diplomacy.

Q. How would you describe bilateral communication between Korea and the U.S., particularly given the latest outcomes of the SMA negotiations?

A. The Special Measures Agreement (SMA), which sets forth measures related to defense cost-sharing between the two allies, has long continued since 1991, with the amount of SMA contributions consistently growing. I would say South Korea is doing what we can to substantially improve the stationing environment for the U.S. and maintain a firm combined defense posture. There were difficulties in the last round of negotiations, but the two sides have never failed to reach an agreement each and every time. I believe it is natural for any allies to go through differences in opinion; EU and NATO are no exceptions. The important thing is for them to coordinate their differences in the wisest, most harmonious and mutually beneficial way.

Q. What would you say are the most distinctive characteristics of diplomacy under the Moon administration?

A. I would call it "A wise, confident approach" with the conventional four — the U.S., China, Japan and Russia, as well as "Diversification" of partners. The Korean government under the current administration has sought to expand smaller-region, multilateral cooperation, such as Korea-China-Japan, Korea-ASEAN and Korea-Visegrad group cooperation. We are also attempting to engage more widely with a diverse global agenda, such as peace-keeping operations (PKO) and official development assistance (ODA), and not just limiting ourselves to NK-related or economic issues. The New Southern Policy under the Moon administration is a good example of such efforts. As this year marks the 30th anniversary of the dialogue partnership between Korea and ASEAN, Korea will be hosting a special Korea-ASEAN Summit. We are also continuing constructive discussions on the establishment of an ASEAN Bureau within the Ministry of Foreign Affairs.

Q. The Korean government is making greater efforts in the area of public diplomacy as well.

A. Today's diplomacy and diplomacy in the future should not just be restricted to government- or ministry-level exchanges. It should aim to win the hearts and minds of the public in Korea, as well as in foreign countries. For this reason, our foreign ministry is making greater efforts to expand the horizon of our diplomatic activities, by not only focusing on the conventional audience of foreign government officials and opinion leaders, but also addressing a wider spectrum of the public in a foreign nation. Our scope of diplomacy will also be widened from the capital cities of the major powers to the local villages of remote countries.

We seek to make the world be better acquainted with our cultural appeal, and more deeply understand our policy initiatives based on Korea's role within the international community. Institutionally, this has been reflected by a steadily growing public diplomacy sector within the foreign ministry.

Q. Any additional comments for our readers?

A. I want to emphasize, on a final note, that the goal of Korean diplomacy, particularly this year, will be to make our diplomatic efforts more engaged with and less distanced from the people's day-to-day lives. Our plans to further enhance mutual cooperation with China on the fine dust issue is a superb example of this.

Also, I would like to underscore the importance of further strengthening our diplomatic capability. I believe there are mainly two ways in which this could be done. One is to enhance the individual capabilities through consistent diplomatic reforms toward increased work productivity. The other is further augmenting our diplomatic infrastructure, such as man-power and resources. These two factors must go hand in hand, as one without the other is like an empty shell. Bearing this in mind, our ministry is sparing no effort to harness authentic reforms and renovations through various initiatives.

Published date: 2019. 04. 06

[REVIEW]

2018 Seoul Defense Dialogue: Overall discourse about the Korean peninsula

By Jaeho Hwang, Professor, Hankuk University of Foreign Studies, Seoul.

The seventh Seoul Defense Dialogue (SDD 2018) was held for three days from September 12-14. This year's SDD resulted in strong debate inside and outside the country, because since it took place right before the Pyongyang Inter-Korean Summit between president Moon Jae-in and Kim Jong-un on Sept. 18.

At the very first SDD, in 2012, there were only 167 participants from 15 countries and two international organizations; but it has steadily grown — this year there were 800 participants from 52 countries and three international organizations.

Participating countries also have expanded from the Asia-Pacific region to Europe, the Middle East, and Africa. Compared to SDD 2012, the number of sessions has risen from three to eight.

At SDD 2018's "Sustainable Peace: From Conflict to Cooperation", there were four plenary sessions: Ⅰ. Denuclearization of the Korean Peninsula and Establishment of a Peace Regime, Ⅱ. Strategic Balance in Northeast Asia. Cooperation and Confidence Building, Ⅲ. Maritime Security Cooperation: Challenges and Tasks, Ⅳ. Cyber Security: Strengthening Mutual Cooperation and four special sessions: Ⅰ. Defense Cooperation for Energy security, Ⅱ. Defense Cooperation for International Peacekeeping Activities, Ⅲ. Defense Cooperation for Prevention of Violent Extremism, Ⅳ. Defense Cooperation for Humanitarian Assistance and Disaster Relief.

Opening ceremony

Korean Minister of National Defense Song Young-moo delivered said in his opening remarks, "We are now standing oat the historical transitioning point where the world's last frontier of the Cold War, the Korean Peninsula, is ending the confrontation and moving toward to peaceful cooperation. Korea is not going to let this opportunity pass by us".

In the keynote address, Korean Director of National Security Chung Eui-yong emphasized that peace was the President Moon government's goal. Therefore, it aimed to eliminate the threat of war from the Korean peninsula by accomplishing complete denuclearization and building a permanent peace regime.

He also said the Inter-Korean Summit (on Sep. 18) would be a big step following the DPRK-U.S. Summit, with both sides striving to reach consensus on building mutual military trust and ending the armed conflict.

Plenary Sessions

In plenary session 1, Seoul National University Professor Emeritus Yoon Young-kwan moderated the topic of denuclearization of the Korean peninsula and building a peace regime.

Korean Vice Minister of Unification Chun Hae-sung said that after the successful DPRK-U.S. Summit, the Korea peninsula was finally ready for denuclearization and a peace regime. Although the DPRK and the U.S. still had different views regarding the sequence of denuclearization and guaranteeing DPRK's political system, the development of inter-Korean relations would contribute on DPRK-U.S. relations as well.

The other presenter, RAND Corporation senior political scientist Andrew Scobell suggested Korea needed to establish its own model for denuclearization because of the difficulties of defining the denuclearization and because of different characteristics to previous cases.

Vice Minister of National Defense Suh Choo-suk pointed that both Koreas' leaders agreed on a steady decrease in military activity leading to military detente, and that trust building would be the core of bringing about permanent peace on the Korean peninsula.

He added that once Korea started its peace and prosperity era, not only Northeast Asia, but the world will soon reap the rewards.

Tsinghua University Vice Director of Institute of Contemporary International Relations Liu Jiangyong said the U.N. Security Council should

reduce the sanctions on the DPRK because only engagement and communication would bring the DPRK to the denuclearization table.

On the other hand, Chancellor of Takushoku University Satoshi Morimoto argued that the sanctions and current defense preparedness must continue until the DPRK's military threats actually decreased.

Feodor Voytolovskiy, Director of the Primakov Institute of World Economy and International Relations (IMEMO) of the Russian Academy of Sciences, noted that international organizations and international society's political, financial, and technological aid would be significant in bringing about ultimate peace on the Korean peninsula.

And finally, Marcel Pesko, Director of the OSCE Conflict Prevention

Centre, suggested that the Helsinki Process must be considered as a long-term project that could be applied to bring about Korean denuclearization.

Plenary session two was moderated by Canadian Global Affairs Institute Vice President Colin Robertson.

Kim Joon-hyung, a professor at Handong Global University said the international order was faltering and the China-U.S. confrontation was getting serious; citing the tension on the Korean peninsula and in the Taiwan straits.

Abraham Denmark, Director of Asia Program at the Woodrow Wilson International Center for Scholars, said the China-U.S. confrontation would be a dilemma for Korea because Korea preferred positive relations with both. However, Korea must keep in mind that the ROK-U.S. alliance was far more important than anything else.

Zhang Tuosheng, Chairman of the Academic Committee of the China Foundation for International Strategic Studies, said ongoing conversation was needed to stabilize relations among the major powers, build international cooperation for Korean denuclearization and peace building, and to resolve maritime and territorial disputes to improve Northeast Asia's strategic balance.

Alexander Nikitin, Director of the Centre for Euro-Atlantic Security at the Moscow State Institute of International Relations, noted that even though Northeast Asia had to deal with multiple security challenges, unlike Europe, it did not have a representative regional institution or treaty for stabilization.

Professor Noboru Yamaguchi from the Japanese International University said China had to keep thinking about how to structure not only regional order but also at international level. It needed to consider how to lead the DPRK into international society as well as providing economic aid.

Randall Schriver, U.S. Assistant Secretary of Defense for Asian and Pacific Security Affairs of, stressed that there was no change in U.S. general policy on Asia and that the U.S. still focused on its traditional alliances.

He also said that trust building with China was one issue; however, managing the situation before it expanded into military conflict was more significant.

William Alberque, Director of NATO's WMD Arms Control, Disarmament, and Non-Proliferation Center, stressed that the bilateral effort was effective only when it came with a multilateral effort. He suggested there should be a practical working group for trust building at next year's SDD.

Plenary session three was moderated by Korea Institute for Maritime Strategy President Lee Seo-hang.

Yeo Suk-joo, Deputy Minister of Defense Policy at the Ministry of National Defense of Korea, highlighted the necessity of cooperation to make the most of the New-Southern Policy and also to bring about peace and prosperity in Asia. He also proposed an 'umbrella' system to manage maritime security.

Euan Graham, Director of the Lowy Institute's International Security Program, specifically analyzed several countries' situations as well as Korea's status as a strategic maritime location.

Pang Zhongying, Dean of the Institute of Marine Development Studies at China's Ocean University, explained China's One Belt One Road, China's maritime policies, and how maritime security based on science and technology would contribute to peace and prosperity.

Dang Quang Minh, Acting Director of Vietnam's Institute of Defense Strategic Studies, said universal cooperation and compliance with international law were necessary.

Canada's Deputy Minister of National Defense Jody Thomas said maritime security needed to be extended in various aspects; for instance, preserving marine life and resources.

Nicolas Regaud, France's Special Representative to the Indo-Pacific of the Directorate General for International Relations and Strategy, also mentioned the environmental perspective as well the importance of nations sharing humanitarian efforts and information.

The Cyber Security session, which Daniel Stauffacher, President of the ICT4 Peace Foundation, moderated, was a new and interesting area at the SDD.

Kwon Hyuk-jin, Director General of the Information Planning Bureau at Korea's Ministry of Defense, said now was the time where cyber military action was demanded, with both advanced detection and information sharing to prevent cyber attack is required.

Ewan Lawson, Senior Research Fellow from the Royal United Services Institute, strongly stressed that building a digital frame was urgent because the world was finding it difficult to understand each other's norms.

Moreover, Professor My Thai from Florida University introduced diverse examples of cyber security issues and pointed out that the higher technology dependency goes, the higher the risk. Lastly, Jun Osawa, Senior Research Fellow from the Nakasone Yasuhiro Peace Institute, focused on the need to develop a cyber security strategy to prevent surprise attacks from state and non-state belligerents.

Special Sessions

Continued, defense cooperation in various sectors was discussed at special sessions.

Kelly Magsamen, Vice President of National Security and International Policy at the Center for American Progress, moderated special session 1, which focused on energy security.

Pak Yong-duk, Managing Director of the Korea Energy Economy Institute, said international cooperation was needed to prevent terror attacks that endangered energy security.

Neil Melvin, Director of the Armed Conflict and Conflict Management Program at the Stockholm International Peace Research Institute said China's increased energy meant the Indian Ocean would be the main transport route. Therefore, the region needed to be secured through multilateral cooperation.

Huan Yunsong, Associate Dean of the School of International Studies at Sichuan University, said China considered energy security a public necessity, so it therefore would cooperate in ensuring energy security.

Prashanth Parameswaran, Senior Editor from The Diplomat, said energy security must be approached from all economic, diplomatic, and security aspects.

Special session 2, about PKO, was moderated by Professor Hong Kyu Dok from Sookmyung Women's University.

Professor Im Yoon-gab from Korea National Defense University, shared his overseas experience over the past 25 years and also explained the need for secured public opinions.

Markus Kaim, Senior Fellow from the German Institute for International and Security Affairs at Stiftung Wissenschaft und Politik of Germany, focused on how simple monitoring of PKO had transformed into a complex and multi-leveled operation, depending on international security circumstances.

Park Sung-ho from the PKO center, stressed the importance of quick reaction capability while Martin Sebastian, Head of Centre for Maritime Security and Diplomacy at the Maritime Institute of Malaysia, concentrated on Northeast and Southeast Asian countries' regional cooperation on PKO.

Yevgeny Ilyin, First Deputy Chief from the Russian Main Directorate for International Military Cooperation, asked for global understanding on how interests could conflict.

Suay Alpay, Turkey's Deputy Secretary of Defense, also emphasized the need to prevent disputes.

Next, Pascal Boniface, Director of the Institute Relations International Strategic, was moderator of special session 3.

Jang Ji-hyang, Director of the Middle East and North Africa Center at the Asan Institute for Policy Studies, and Charithie Joaquin, from the Research and Special Studies Division at the National Defense College of the Philippines, both emphasized the significance of prevention and response to violent extremism and pointed how governments were facing difficulties in dealing with extremists' rapidly changing tactics.

Muhammad Rifqi Muna, Senior Researcher at the Indonesian Institute of Science Center for Political Studies, was concerned about violent extremist groups' being able to breach cyber security, and their use of SNS to recruit members.

EU Ambassador to Korea Michael Reiterer said that understanding what motivated extremists was the key to understanding and countering terrorism.

Rakesh Bhadauria, Distinguished Fellow at the United Service Institution, moderated special session four, which Associate Research Fellow Liu Shu from China's Academy of Military Science presented.

David Capie, Director of the Center for Strategic Studies at Victoria University of Wellington particularly mentioned military's HADR within the climate change.

Alexander Neill, Senior Fellow at the International Institute for Strategic Studies, Swedish Ambassador Jakob Hallgren, and Sarmiento Beltran, Deputy Secretary of Mexico Navy all strongly supported the need for international strategic cooperation for HADR, and the appropriate response to recipient countries and regional demands.

Concluding Remarks

Seoul Defense Dialogue 2018 enabled us to think deeply about Korea's geopolitical destiny resulting from its division and conflict for the last 70 years. Korea persistently tries to find domestic and international connections to build a peace regime and accomplish denuclearization. The great journey toward peace on the Korean peninsula — a step toward global peace and security — is on the move, and the Seoul Defense Dialogue is part of this.

Published date: 2018. 09. 29